Joachim Kuch

Volkswagen

Model Documentation

Volkswagen

Model Documentation

Beetle to 412, Including Transporter
(Boxer Engine Models)

Joachim Kuch

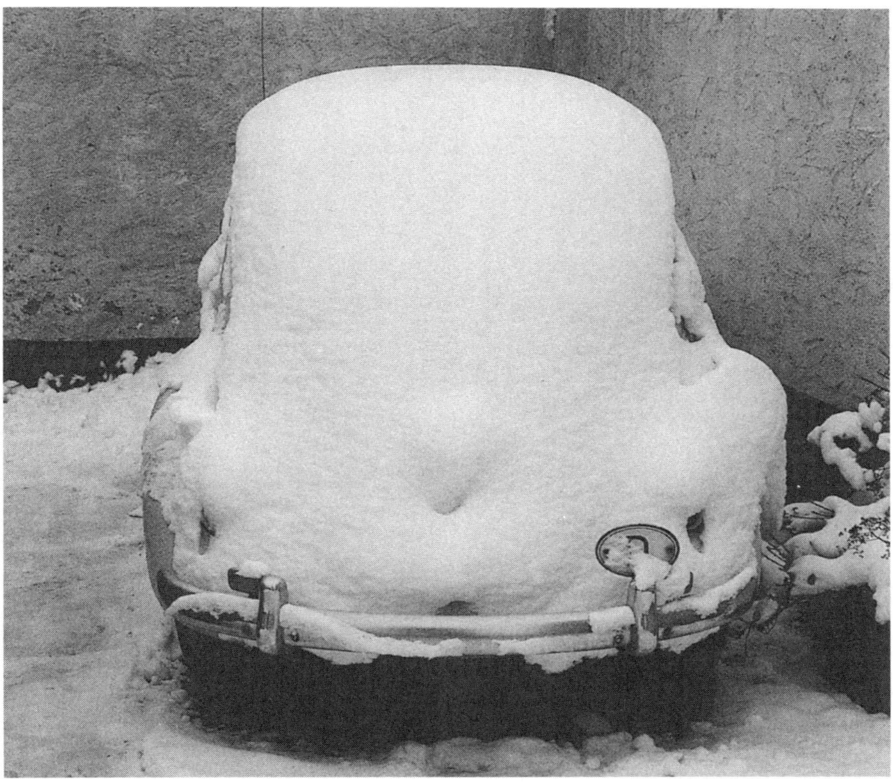

RB
ROBERT BENTLEY
PUBLISHERS

Contents

Exporting began on August 8, 1947, when the Dutch Pon brothers became the first general importers. Page 18

Off the assembly line every 30 seconds: VW production 1958. Page 29

Volkswagen-Porsche Austria prepared 1302S Beetles for use as rally cars. Page 76

Transporter predecessor: the Plattenwagen, based on sketches made by Ivan Hirst and built on the Type 1 platform. Page 139

The 'Tristar' was the luxury version of the double cab including all wheel-drive. Page 174

The VW 411 was available with two and four doors. Both came with a rear engine which provided certain advantages in the winter. Page 223

RB ROBERT BENTLEY, INC. | AUTOMOTIVE PUBLISHERS

Information that makes the difference.®

1734 Massachusetts Avenue
Cambridge, MA 02138 USA
800-423-4595 / 617-547-4170
e-mail: sales@rb.com
www.rb.com

Copies of this book may be purchased from selected booksellers, or directly from the publisher by mail. The publisher encourages comments from the reader of this book. Please write to Robert Bentley, Inc., Publishers at the address listed on the top of this page.

Library of Congress Cataloging-in-Publication Data

Kuch, Joachim.
[Volkswagen Modellgeschichte. English]
Volkswagen model documentation: Beetle to 412, including Transporter (boxer engine models)/Joachim Kuch.
p.cm.
ISBN 0-8376-0078-2 (alk. Paper)
1. Volkswagen automobiles—History. 2. Volkswagen automobiles—Specifications. I. Title.

TL215.V6 K8313 1999
629.222'2—dc21

99-045688

ISBN: 0-8376-0078-2
Bentley Stock No. GVM1

02 01 00 99 10 9 8 7 6 5 4 3 2 1

(∞) The paper used in this publication is acid free and meets the requirements of the National Standard for Information Sciences-Permanence of Paper for Printed Library Materials.

Manufactured in the United States of America

Translator: Erik S. Meyers

Foreword

I don't exactly come from a family of Volkswagen enthusiasts. My parents' first car was a Lloyd LP 400. In 1963, they bought a Ford Taunus. We didn't have a VW until much later. My father's sons made up for this. Everyone one of them can look back on many special Beetle experiences. My own are a mixed lot of both good and bad. For example, when I took my motorcycle license test, an old man used his old Beetle to get me out of my seat at an intersection. During my military service, I usually drove around in a Mexican-built Beetle. The clutch was absolutely terrible and didn't always engage all the way-or even at all. This made for a bumpy ride that came with indignant comments from the decorated military man in the back seat trying to read the paper. Our chief mechanic said this was completely normal for a Mexican-built Beetle. Whether it was the clutch or my driving skills, it didn't matter; I hated that thing.

My brother's third open-air Beetle, a red 1303 Cabriolet, made up for that. Twelve years ago he drove my then girlfriend, Ulrike, and me to the altar in it. The four of us are still together. This book is definitely due to that mars-red Karmann four-seater. It must also be said, though, that many kind people contributed to its success.

I would first like to thank Dr. Hans-Rüdiger Etzold, Randolph Unruh, Halwart Schrader and Hans Joachim Klersy. They kept a watchful eye on the manuscript and generously supported me. In addition, the following people also provided invaluable help: Dr. Bernd Wiersch and Eckberth von Witzleben from the Stiftung AutoMuseum Wolfsburg, Mr. Parr and Mr. Thorner from the Porsche AG archive as well as Martin Roland from the Mercedes-Benz Classic. Many thanks also to Katharina and Paul Jüssen, to Wilfried Kaulen for his expert support, to Jörg Austen for his help with the chapter on the VW/Porsche 914, to Claus-Jürgen Jacobsen for photographs, to my mother for her copy editing-and to my wife, for her patience, and for getting into the red 1303 with the sand-colored roof with me 12 years ago.

Joachim Kuch

The King of Wolfsburg: Chairman Dr. h.c. Heinz Nordhoff (January 6, 1899-April 12, 1968).

Chapter 1

The Nordhoff Era

Auto, Motor und Sport called him the "first salesperson at the Volkswagen factory." The American press named him "Mr. Volkswagen," and *Der Spiegel* even went so far as to crown him "King of Wolfsburg." Heinrich Nordhoff, the engineer from Hildesheim near Hanover, never designed or assembled one bolt on a Volkswagen—but without him, there would never have been a Beetle.

The Miracle of Wolfsburg

The idea of building a Volkswagen (a "people's car") had been around for a long time, without ever having been really supported. In 1930s Germany, however, the National Socialists took it upon themselves to make this idea a reality and thus started one of the biggest propaganda campaigns in history. Professor Ferdinand Porsche designed a car in the mid-1930s that was to be mass-produced in a brand-new factory and sold for 999 marks by 1940. The factory for the "KdF" car (KdF stood for "Kraft durch Freude," or "strength through joy," and for the attempt by the state to organize free time for the Germans) was built not far from Fallersleben on the expropriated estate of the Count of Schulenburg. On this sparsely populated land in the heart of Germany, where the Wolfsburg (Wolf castle) once stood, a factory began to take form after 1938. The KdF City to be built for the 50,000 workers was still just a drawing on the architect's drawing board.

The war ended on April 12, 1945, in the KdF City, when the Americans, under Colonel Kennedy, marched into the city. They stopped the plundering and destruction of the factory, set up an engine repair shop, and waited for the British, who, according to the Treaty of Yalta, had responsibility for the northern German occupation zone. The British arrived at the beginning of May, with Major Ivan Hirst making his first appearance in August. His job was to get a production line going as fast as possible. According to Allied plans, 40,000 cars were allowed to be built in Germany for the needs of the occupying troops. Half of these cars were to be built in the British zone. Theoretically, the Ford factory in Cologne could also have been used, but that was not possible. Ambi-Budd, the company that

Wolfsburg 1945-46: After the Americans left, the British took over running the factory in May 1945. The "Wolfsburg Motor Works" was now building cars for the Allies.

supplied body shells for Ford passenger cars before the war, was in the Soviet-occupied part of Berlin and therefore was unable to ship anything. This left only the Wolfsburg factory. One of the first official acts of the occupying powers was to change the name of KdF City to Wolfsburg. The factory was now called the Wolfsburg Motor Works. The Motor Works had lost a lot in the war and only the metal presses for the KdF sedans were still usable.

Automobile production began again with 45 machine tools, including not more than 23 presses. In comparison, the Opel factory in Brandenburg, opened in 1936, only a quarter of the size of the KdF factory and the most modern factory in the pre-war period, had 1,200 machine tools. A new Opel Kadett came off the assembly line every two minutes. During the war, an Opel Blitz was produced every ten minutes.

But Wolfsburg after the war was a different story. Sixty percent of the factory was destroyed. The first bombing in April 1943 turned the 860,000 sq. ft assembly hall into a mound of debris and ash. In the rear of hall 1 was the wreck of an American bomber. During the war, the plan was to build around half a million KdF sedans in the building starting in 1940. However, only 630 Volkswagens and 65,000 Kübel- and Schwimmwagens were actually built. Automobile production only used the smaller section within the huge factory encompassing 40 football fields. The rest of the building was used to build airplane parts and the components for the

View from the main administration building to the parking lot in front of it. One Beetle, one Kübelwagen, two Mercedes 170V and a Tatra 87. The Tatra was the official car for Ivan Hirst and his officer colleagues.

Congratulated on his birthday (May 1, 1946) by the VW workers as the "man who saved the Volkswagen factory": Major Ivan Hirst of the Royal Electrical and Mechanical Engineers (REME).

miracle weapons, V1 and V2. Besides these, no other armaments were built in Wolfsburg. This saved the very expensive metal presses used for the KdF cars from being dismantled. The KdF cars themselves also survived, as they were walled in. As cars for the occupying troops had to be built, the military administration forbade any dismantling for the next four years.

In the year the war ended, 1945, 917 Volkswagen sedans were actually built. In March 1946, the construction of the 1000th Volkswagen was proudly recorded. Production, though, was still far behind the goals set by the military. They had hoped to be building 4000 cars a month by the beginning of 1946. By combining British and German resources, the 20,000 cars got built and the order was filled.

At attention: The first Volkswagens for the occupying troops. These are the type 51 cars: the body came from the KdF car, the chassis from the type 82, the Kübelwagen.

The appointed time to transfer the factory back into German hands was also getting closer. Dismantling was no longer under discussion in the western occupation zones. There were interested parties though; the Australians would have liked to have had the KdF cars. The Soviets, whose zone ended a few kilometers east of Wolfsburg, would have readily sent their dismantling crews. But they were not allowed to; and the Americans didn't want to. Supposedly, Henry Ford II had turned it down when he saw how close the Soviet zone was. Even France had toyed with the idea, although what most were interested in was not the product (a British commission had called the car "old-fashioned, not suitable") but the gigantic production facility with its approximately one-mile-long assembly hall. The British administrators began looking for the right person to take over. If this person didn't actually work out, Ivan Hirst was always available to jump in if needed.

For Hirst, the ideal candidate was Heinrich Nordhoff, for whom mass production was nothing new. In 1942 he had been appointed head of the Opel factory in Brandenburg, the largest truck factory in Europe. However, Brandenburg was now in the Soviet occupation zone. Nordhoff was now making a living as a mechanic and service advisor in a Hamburg garage. A return to Opel for the former head was impossible. The Americans wanted nothing to do with the man who provided the German army with trucks.

Nordhoff, born in 1899, was the son of a private banker in Hildesheim and graduated from the technical college in Brunswick. He was originally supposed to be appointed production manager under Ivan Hirst, but during his interview, Nordhoff, a manager trained by General Motors, impressed Hirst so much that he was offered the job of chairman. The original person in the position, Dr. Münch, a Berlin divorce lawyer, was unencumbered by politics. He had been appointed by the Americans, but knew very little about cars.

Nordhoff hesitated. He had supposedly already decided not to accept the position when he found out that a return to Opel was impossible. But Nordhoff reluctantly took the job with one important condition: he had to be given absolute freedom. The rebuilding and reorganization of the factory was his responsibility alone. Nordhoff said ten years later, "When I was appointed chairman of the Volkswagen factory, I had the right to specify certain conditions. One of these was that I did not want any influence or inter-

At the beginning of 1946, the CCG cars (Control Commission for Germany) were presented to the British military at the VW factory in Fallersleben. The cars were inspected carefully. At first the rear engine concept was too much for the drivers, as they were not used to the way the Beetle handled. This, together with the poor road conditions, led to many accidents.

ference from anyone. I didn't have a contract and I didn't know anything about the factory or the product. I literally had to start from scratch. Seven thousand workers toiled to build 6000 cars a year depending, of course, on how much it rained. The roof and all of the windows had been destroyed."

The bombed-out hall 3 is shown here. The car floor pans were built in hall 2 where engine bench testing was done.

Nordhoff's Maxims: Quality & Mass Production

The liaison between Nordhoff and VW was a marriage of reason not love. The comments from the new chairman were not exactly flattering. He called the Volkswagen "a small, cheap thing," with "more defects than a dog had fleas." And he was right, at least in terms of the Beetles built in 1946-47. At that time the factory lacked many parts, including glass for the windows (any glass produced was first used for houses), adhesives (isinglass, which stank in the heat, was sometimes used), steel for the bodies, and carburetor parts (the only source was a camera manufacturer in Brunswick). Basically, the first Beetles were uncomfortable, loud, and of poor quality. There was something special about the cars though. Something that even satisfied someone like Heinrich Nordhoff, among others: "This is not your run-of-the-mill car, as many cars

After 65% of the factory was destroyed, the 700 factory workers in Wolfsburg had their hands full getting rid of the rubble. They would not have been able to do it without British help. On the right is a Scammell 6 x 4 that the British engineers used to carry away the debris. On the left, what was left of the war production facility: wings with engine carriers, probably for a Dornier.

these days are, assembled as if by magic. This automobile is a personality." He found it "with a mind of its own as well as unusual," if not at least a little cantankerous.

But that all changed quickly, as the first measures to build a car with at least a minimum of driving comfort were put into place. For a car man who had learned from an American company, this made a lot of sense. The test department under Rudolf Ringel, who had developed the two- and four-seater Cabriolets and the Plattenwagen under British direction, could definitely not complain about boredom anymore. Under Nordhoff, Volkswagen began a model improvement plan more systematic than any other manufacturer. By 1953, the company could boast more than 400 measures and improvements compared to the first post-war cars. By 1962, an ad in the magazine *Quick Ende* talked about 2064 improvements.

Heinrich Nordhoff was someone who quickly came to the point. This included his speech to the Volkswagen employees when he took over running the plant: "This year, for the first time in history, the Volkswagen factory must be able to stand on its own two feet. Right now, it takes 700 man-hours to build a car. If we continue like this, we won't continue for very long. We must be able to build a car in 100 hours." Within five months, Nordhoff had tightened and streamlined the procedures.

Before the currency reform, many components were obtained by barter. Nordhoff's factory only managed to survive the currency reform by "pulling strings" (*Der Spiegel*). The VW factory had no cash; bank credit wasn't possible due to the question of who actually owned the company. But Nordhoff managed to pull through anyway. His decision: cars paid for by cash in advance. This actually worked; more than one dealer came to Wolfsburg with a briefcase full of brand new deutsche mark (DM) bills. VW used this money to build the most sought-after post-war product: Volkswagens.

In 1948, the year King Heinrich was crowned, Volkswagen built 19,127 cars. Opel built 5762 Olympias and 266 Kapitäns. In the entire country, a total of only 30,751 passenger cars were built that year. But this number improved. In 1949, VW built 46,590 units. Opel in Rüsselsheim produced 27,990 Olympias and Kapitäns. Records kept being broken. When Wolfsburg announced they had built 6003 cars in April 1950, the magazine *Der Spiegel* wasn't the only one to ask, "Where are all these cars going to go?" This question was answered by the customers: a new Beetle came off the assembly line every two minutes, and there were still waiting times of several months.

Each month, 430 train cars arrived in Wolfsburg, bringing with them sheet steel and casting parts, rubber, paint, and electronic components; 650 cars brought almost 10,000 metric tons of coke and coal from the Ruhr area to feed the massive power plant. Those were the figures from 1949 found in Heinz Todtmann's book *Kleiner Wagen auf grosser Fahrt* (Small Car on a Long Journey). At that time, 4000 cars left the assembly halls per month. By 1953, 250 train cars were emptied daily, with a total production of 180,047 cars that year. In July, the plant built the 500,000th Beetle. The Wolfsburg company was the largest automobile manufacturer in

No roof over their heads, but cars were built. According to the Allied agreement, the British were to direct the production of 20,000 Volkswagens. In addition to cars, roofs and cabins were built for Ford in 1948.

Automobile production quickly got back up to speed. By March 1950, monthly Volkswagen production had already risen to 6317 cars. In May, after production of the Type 2 started, 7000 vehicles were built.

Germany. The next largest was Opel, with 105,792 units. In third place was Mercedes-Benz with 51,660 cars. Ford was in fourth; compared to its 182 Taunus cars built in 1948, Ford now produced 44,009 vehicles.

In 1950, 515 cars were built per working day; by 1954 this number increased to 1048. The daily average in 1958 (13 years after the war ended), was 2402 units. This number had doubled to 5250 cars only five years later.

There is no shortage of attempts to explain this gigantic success. Even though other managers in the industry had certainly done their homework, the passionate big-game hunter, Nordhoff, became the leader of the entire industry. That this loner, who started at BMW in 1929 with a salary of DM 140 per month and left VW as chairman with a yearly salary of around a million DM, didn't make many friends was inevitable. As early as 1949 the unions accused him of an "autocratic and dictatorial" management style. Many people considered him a gambler. It also seemed as if the "genius of Wolfsburg" (*Der Spiegel*) suffered from delusions of grandeur. The press quoted him as saying, "Germany should go where Volkswagen leads it, not the other way around."

At the end of 1950, VW was accused of blindly clinging to the air-cooled engine in the rear while ignoring technical progress. On the other hand, it was this unerring belief in the Porsche concept

that made the Volkswagen such a success. That, and the fact that Nordhoff placed such great importance on exporting the cars, even though the demand in Germany was far from being satisfied. Many people waited 10, 12, or even 14 months for a car at the end of the 1950s. Volkswagens weren't sold, they were distributed.

The high degree of automation also had to do with the turnover of personnel during the early years. At the end of 1947 there were 8382 employees. That year the company had hired 3921 people, and 3800 had left. Wages were at the level they had been in 1936. The work-week was 42.5 hours, and there were even attempts to introduce a 48-hour workweek.

Who Owned Volkswagen?

Until 1960, it was unclear who actually owned the Volkswagen factory. The pre-WWII Volkswagen factory with headquarters in Berlin was a company founded by the Deutsche Arbeitsfront (DAF) (German Work Front). The DAF held all the shares through the Vermügensverwaltung der DAF GmbH (Property Administration of DAF Ltd.) and the Treuhandverwaltung für die wirtschaftlichen Unternehmungen der DAF GmbH (Trust Administration for the Economic Enterprises of DAF Ltd.). After 1945, these companies were dissolved, but the Volkswagen factory lived on and was under British control until the autumn of 1949. Decree 202 transferred the factory to the newly founded Federal Republic of Germany. The federal minister of trade and commerce placed it in the care of the Minister of Trade and Commerce of Lower Saxony, Fricke. And he was the person who managed Nordhoff. An advisor for the VW factory was named in 1951. On paper, Heinrich Nordhoff had two

With Decree 202 on September 8, 1949, the Federal Republic of Germany became owner of the Volkswagen factory. Charles R. Radclyffe, Ivan Hirst's boss, signed for the British. Standing on the right with glasses in hand, Law Professor Ludwig Erhard, who was to be named Minister of Trade and Commerce two weeks later. Standing on the left, is, presumably, the representative of the government of Lower Saxony.

other managers on the side. There was never a doubt, though, who kept the VW ship on its successful course.

Finally, in July 1960, the federal and state governments cleared up the question of ownership. The "Volkswagen bill" made it possible to regulate the legal circumstances and establish a Stiftung Volkswagen (Volkswagen Foundation). The GmbH (limited company) became an AG (corporation). The capital was increased from 300 million DM to 600 million DM: 20% each for the state and federal governments, the other 60% was distributed as stock. For political reasons, the price was set at 360 DM per 100 DM share (extremely undervalued according to stockbrokers). Oversubscribed multiple times, the shares finally had to be distributed. As of August 22, 1960, around 1.3 million small shareholders could consider themselves part owners of the largest automobile

Public stock: With the privatization of Volkswagen, the stock was oversubscribed many times. The rate of issue was set at 360 marks—half the price people would have paid on the open market. VW employees got preferential treatment when the stock was issued. This led to some legal battles.

manufacturer. These were the best VW customers. Many of them were veterans of the war, people who had seen what the Kübelwagen could do. "The Kübelwagen was driven on the longest test run of all times, this vehicle is at home in the desert as well as in the mud," wrote Heinz Kranz, senior editor of the magazine *automobil technik und sport*, in February 1959. During the war he was head of a repair unit, "responsible for keeping hundreds of these things ready for action."

Every child knew that a Volkswagen was reliable. If there was a problem, there was a garage on every corner. The first 24 Volkswagen garages were opened in 1946 as repair shops for the occupying forces. By 1950 there were around 600 dealers in Germany; by 1955 this number had risen to 1000. Ten years later, there were almost 3000 (2972, to be exact). Running a VW dealership was a sure thing, with recognizable overhead. In addition, the one-model policy used until 1961 simplified planning and parts supplies for dealers. The VW enjoyed a trust that others still had to earn. While competitors' ads said, "Opel, the Reliable Car," Volkswagen did not need to say that.

The ever-increasing numbers spoke for themselves. In 1955, 279,986 type 1 Beetles were built. The one millionth Volkswagen rolled off the assembly line on August 5 of that year. The city of Wolfsburg made the VW boss an honorary citizen. Just before that,

Exporting began on August 8, 1947, when the Dutch Pon brothers became the first general importers. Pon and his brothers took delivery of their first six cars on October 16.

The two millionth Beetle rolled off the assembly line on December 28, 1957, at 2:35 p.m. That year, Volkswagen produced 470,000 cars; 270,000 of those were for export.

Nordhoff had been awarded an honorary professorship. The German government conferred the Order of the Federal Republic of Germany on Nordhoff, in particular due to his contribution to German exports; the Volkswagen factory was the largest earner of foreign currency. Business in the US, in particular, was flourishing.

Success in the US

While he was at Opel, Heinrich Nordhoff learned about the US relationship to the automobile. On the other side of the ocean, owning a car was a given. In the mid-1930s, one in five Americans owned a car. In Germany at the time, there was one car for every 500 citizens.

The first export VWs were 56 Beetle sedans that Ivan Hirst transferred to the Dutch exporter, Ben Pon, in 1947. Pon had to wait until he had enough replacement parts to move them to Holland. He came to Wolfsburg, dressed in the Dutch uniform, with his brothers. Pon, as a civilian, had already tried to get a VW import license back in 1939.

Ben Pon was also the person who, on January 8, 1949, shipped a gray export Beetle from Rotterdam to New York. But, unfortunately, he was unable to find any interested dealers. Nordhoff, who traveled to the US three months later, had the same result. He didn't

have any cars with him, only photographs and brochures, but no one was interested in these either. Finally, Maximilian "Maxie" Edwin Hoffmann took on the Beetle. Maxie was from Vienna and had come to the US at the beginning of the war. In 1946 he opened a European car dealership in New York. Sports cars such as the Mercedes SL, Porsche Speedster, and BMW 507 were due to his suggestions. Between 1950 and 1954, Hoffmann Motors Corporation handled Beetle imports. In the first year, 157 Beetles took to the American highways. In 1951, 390 were sold; in 1952, 601. The next year, 980 were sold. Within this period, 2173 Beetles and 43 vans were sold in the US.

At the end of the year, the agreement between VW and the most successful American car dealer of all time ended. The man with a nose for sport cars was never able to build a countrywide service organization. After the contract was canceled, independent importers took over for the next two years. Thanks in part to the favorable DM/dollar exchange rate, they managed to sell around 24,000 Volkswagens. Heinrich Nordhoff took over from there: On July 21, 1955, in the New York St. Moritz hotel, he founded Volkswagen United States, Inc. A factory was bought in New Brunswick, New Jersey, as it was thought they might build Beetles in the US. But wage costs were too high, so they sold the production facility.

In the mid-1960s, Volkswagen chartered 68 specially built ships with a total of 550,000 gross metric tons. This weight was 12% of the total German freight tonnage.

"A member of the family" that just happens to live in the garage: A VW ad from around 1963.

New Brunswick became the headquarters of Volkswagen of America (VWoA) which took over from Volkswagen United States on October 27, 1955, with $100,000 in capital. Imports were administered through two regional offices. The office for the East Coast was in New York, with the office for the West Coast in San Francisco. Nordhoff gave the job of building a dealer network to two of his most capable employees, Gottfried Lange and Will van de Kamp. Very quickly, there were 15 distributors and 342 dealers. By 1955, 35,851 Volkswagens (including 2000 vans) had been sold without any advertising. As a comparison, the total sales of all foreign car importers that year was 51,000. In 1957, VW sold 75,000 units; in 1959 this number was 135,000. Nothing seemed to be able to stop the flood of Beetles. The Americans loved this car, the opposite of American cars at the time. The Beetle was everything the

Even available in Germany, albeit as a special reprint: what Americans like about the Beetle.

cars from Detroit were not: noisy, slow, small, but also inexpensive to buy and maintain.

In terms of service, reliability, and stability of value, the Volkswagen was alone at the top. According to the December 1959 issue of *Populäre Mechanik* (*Popular Mechanics*), a two-year-old Beetle was still worth 81% of its original value. A Renault Dauphine, on the other hand, was only worth 50% of its original value. *Der Spiegel* wrote about American buyers who came to Germany regularly to buy used Volkswagens at inflated prices and then sell them in the US at a huge profit. One in every five Beetles registered in the US between 1958 and 1960 was a gray-market car.

Heinrich Nordhoff was also a success in the US. His greatest satisfaction was when he won the Elmer A. Sperry prize, along with the Wolfsburg team and Ferdinand Porsche. Porsche, the man who created the Volkswagen, had died in 1951. The Sperry prize was something like the Nobel prize for engineers. The year 1958 was the first time it had been awarded to someone within the automobile industry, "for developing the Volkswagen, a small car designed and built for multiple uses. This car is for everyone, with low acquisition and operating costs and simple construction. It is easy to repair and provides comfort for satisfactory performance. Fuel economy is ideal for both the city and the countryside."

Nordhoff traveled to New York to personally accept the award on November 13, 1958. He later called that day, "the most beautiful day of my life." During his acceptance speech, the professor offered his recipe for success: "a product of the highest quality, with low purchase price and an incomparable resale value." This is

The Sperry prize was only one of the many honors awarded Nordhoff. The prize also went to Ferdinand Porsche and the Volkswagen employees.

exactly what made the car such a success, not just in Germany but also in the US.

The phenomenal success was also due to the fact that a 1954 Beetle looked almost identical to a 1960 Beetle. The Beetle was timeless and didn't belong to just one class; not something American cars (which were also much larger and cost several hundred dollars more) at the time could boast. The Detroit cars changed every year. Anyone driving a three-year-old American model was immediately identified as someone who couldn't afford the latest and greatest. But those that drove around in Beetles weren't part of that.

In the December 1956 issue of *Popular Mechanics* Floyd Clymer described why Americans were fascinated by the Beetle. A special edition of that flattering report was even translated into German: "With a 2400 mm (94 inch) wheelbase, this small, short car is very stable and sure on the road. This is what astounds the average American driver. This German car boasts impressive driving characteristics." With a displacement "similar to our heavy motorcycles," his conclusion was: "In my opinion, the Volkswagen is a practical, reliable car, suitable for anybody who needs a cheap means of transportation. Almost every driver of a Volkswagen is an unpaid spokesperson. Most of them are always ready to sing the praises of their car." To support this assertion, a survey in which "hundreds of VW owners" took part was included in the issue immediately following the article.

According to the poll, 95.8% of VW owners rated their cars "excellent." Of course the very good price of $1600 (DM 6720) must have played a part: 68.9% of buyers chose the VW because it was so economical. A retired man in New Jersey said, "My V8 used to cost me $3.50 to $4.00 a week in fuel. Now I only spend between $0.90 and $1.00." A bank teller from California calculated that he had spent only $51.00 (DM 214) on operating costs for a 5000 mile (8000 km) trip. This included fuel, two lubrications and an oil change (with a car wash). There were also critics among those who responded. They criticized the "engine and transmission noise," as well as the "limited views to the front and rear." Critics were definitely in the minority, though. Whereas 10% of the respondents were dissatisfied, 25.9% saw no reason to change anything. Thus the special reprint, which was not done just as a VW advertisement, ended just as it had started, with songs of praise, echoed by an unnamed model builder from Ohio: "The best small car I ever sat in. You can push the car to the limit and not have to worry. If I ever need a second car, it will definitely be another Volkswagen."

By the middle of the 1960s VW had definitely recouped its initial $250 million investment in building a service network. The US had been the biggest export market for quite some time. At the end of 1963, there were 750 VW centers in the United States. In 1964,

In 1959, Heinrich "Heinz" Nordhoff (center) appointed Carl H. Hahn (left) to run the US subsidiary. Hahn, who would later become head of VW, had a decisive role in the success of the export business. He hired the DDB ad agency, which designed a completely new advertising style. By the end of 1967, three million VWs had been sold in North America.

these centers took care of around 1.4 million Volkswagens. Volkswagens were also particularly plentiful in Sweden (375,000), the Netherlands (280,000), Canada (265,000), Switzerland (225,000), Belgium (225,000), Austria (195,000), Denmark (150,000) and Italy (147,000). Of the 537,145 import cars sold in the US in 1965, 357,143 came from Wolfsburg. US dealers sold an average of 25,000 Volkswagens a month. Driving a Beetle was definitely "in." Which is exactly what brought the American ad agency Doyle Dane Bernbach (DDB) such success.

DDB wasn't your normal advertising agency, which is why they had gotten the contract in 1959. They were a small, unconventional group, but they were imaginative. Their ads did away with the lifestyle shots the other ad agencies produced: in front of the opera or the photographs gleaming with chrome. Their approach was to use slogans that spoke to the people with a wink. The DDB

Most ships used in 1973 to transport cars were chartered, although VW had three specially built ships of their own. Export numbers were steadily falling, though. In 1970, VW sold 504,600 cars in the US, corresponding to a market share of 6.1%. Five years later, the number of cars sold dropped to 246,200, only 2.8% market share.

campaigns were certainly successful. In 1966, Americans bought 420,000 Volkswagens. This was more than a quarter of VW's yearly production. By 1967, this number had risen to 449,354. The best Beetle year ever was 1968, with 390,379 Beetles and 9,595 Beetle convertibles sold. All in all, Americans bought 569,292 Volkswagens.

At the end of the 1960s, Volkswagen's power over the American continent seemed to be diminishing. In 1969, VW sold 40,000 cars less than the year before, while Nissan, Toyota, and others had managed to adapt their product better to American tastes. Their cars were also not much more expensive than a Volkswagen and they put Volkswagen more on the defensive. By 1973, Volkswagen's import market share dropped dramatically from an unbelievable 62% down to 46%. Whatever VW lost, Datsun and Toyota gained. In 1975, Toyota overtook Volkswagen as the largest importer.

From the People's Car to a Car for the People

During the war, around 630 KdF cars were built, none of which ever made it into the hands of the public. After the war, things pretty much stayed the same. The new KdF car was still called a

"Volkswagen," but it was anything but a car for the people. "The names Volkswagen and Volkswagen factory should only be allowed to be used when any German citizen can own one," said the Hilfsverein ehemaliger Volkswagensparer (Support Society for Former Volkswagen Savers). Statistically, the average worker earned a net monthly salary of DM 213 in 1950. It would have taken 493 days to earn enough for a Volkswagen. "If the idea of a people's car is no longer attainable, this isn't due to the design, but rather to the fact that we are living in a completely different time. Thoughts and ideas are free of any unwarranted optimism. The people who run VW today are well aware that they had abandoned the original goal," said the magazine *Der Motorsport + Motorradwelt* in their February 1950 issue.

The real Volkswagens (people's cars) at the time were at first small motorcycles, mopeds, and scooters. By the middle of the decade, there was the Isetta, Messerschmitt and Lloyd, Victoria

If you had a full savings book, you would be able to enjoy a KdF car—in theory at least. None of the VW savers ever actually got a car. The validity of these books was later tested during the 12-year VW saver's trial.

Spatz, and Fuldamobile. The letter pages of the relevant magazines contained many opinions about the ideal mini car, pictures of cars people had built themselves, as well as tips for determining costs for do-it-yourselfers. By the end of the decade, when the three millionth Volkswagen rolled off the assembly line on August 25, 1959, the situation had changed dramatically. The average income had doubled in ten years to DM 432 per month (1960). It would now have taken only 174 days to earn enough money for a Volkswagen. And if you were one of the lucky people who still owned a full KdF savings book from the Nazi era, you could get a considerable discount on a VW 1200.

The Volkswagen Savings Case

The Volkswagen savings case had begun in July 1949. When it ended in October 1961 it was the longest case in post-war Germany. The first court date had lasted seven minutes, the final one ten hours. In between lay 12 years, nine trials, and costs as high as around half a million deutsche marks.

The roots of the "monster trial" (*Der Spiegel*) lay in the Third Reich. Back then, every citizen (women had to get their husband's signature) was to be able to own a KdF car as long as they had collected the required savings stamps. Until 1945, 336,000 people saved, counted, and glued, but after 1945 were staring at an empty jar. With the Third Reich no more, those savings books were worthless.

Around 40,000 of these savers organized themselves into the Hilfsverein ehemaligen Volkswagensparer (Support Society for Former Volkswagen Savers). Two of them, Karl Stolz and Rudolf

Patriarch: Even if not always loved, Nordhoff was respected as a strict but fair father. Although the unions were soon holding his style of leadership against him, there was still cooperation between the two. Hugo Bork (center) was the first chair of the factory committee and there for many years. The cooperation between him and Nordhoff (here at a companywide meeting in 1960) was one of the reasons the company was so successful.

Off the assembly line every 30 seconds: VW production 1958. In Emden in 1964, VW opened another factory to meet the increasing demand. This factory built cars for export.

Meichsner, had saved 1310 reichsmarks and 875 reichsmarks respectively. They sued the Volkswagen factory on behalf of the others for delivery of a Volkswagen, demanding that Volkswagen fully accept all payments made during the KdF years. The first court date was July 7, 1949, in front of the county court in Hildesheim. The Volkswagen representatives raised an objection, as they had supposedly not received the documents in time. The next hearing in January 1950 was also a loss for the VW savers (the court gave many reasons including the fact that the VW factory would go bankrupt if everyone who had a savings book were to receive a Beetle at a special discount). In appeal, the VW savers were also left empty-handed. The Court of Appeals in Celle was of the opinion that the VW savers had a contract with the Deutsche Arbeitsfront (DAF, the German Worker Front) and not with Volkswagen.

Stolz and Meichsner then took their case to the Supreme Court in Karlsruhe and had a partial success. The decision from the previous trial was reversed. The Supreme Court first wanted to know how many savers actually wanted to get a car. The Supreme Court justices did not make a decision then about whether the VW savers should be suing the DAF or the VW factory. They didn't decide this until December 1954. That trial was due to Volkswagen's attorneys, who stated that there were no contract or obligations between the savers and the factory. Karl Stolz was stubborn and refused any settlement. Volkswagen offered a DM 500 discount or DM 250 cash settlement for anyone who had a full savings book.

In 1961, when both parties made the trek to Karlsruhe for the fourth time, they came to a mutual agreement in the chambers of the Supreme Court. This stated that anyone who had a full book would receive the maximum discount of DM 600 on a new VW. Even someone who had only saved a fourth of the sum required did not go away empty-handed. They received DM 150 off a VW 1200. Some also got a cash settlement ranging from DM 25 to 100. Nordhoff also paid for a part of the society's legal costs and promised to reserve 12,000 Beetles a year for VW savers. By the June 1953 deadline, 130,000 VW savers had registered. In the worst case, savers would have to wait 10 years for "their" Volkswagen.

Both sides could live with the settlement. VW was also able to use money from the DAF account, frozen since the end of the war. The balance was 300 million reichsmarks, which still came to around DM 15 million. VW's balance sheet for December 31, 1960, also referenced DM 242 million for "reserves for various unknown debts." The VW savers had not been an economic threat for VW for quite a while. However, the time had definitely come to find an ideal successor for the Beetle.

The Search for a Beetle Replacement

Calls for a successor to the Beetle had begun as early as the middle of the 1950s. The media was full of speculation about what the successor would look like. Until the new car was actually announced, there were a number of design contests. *Road & Track*, one of the leading American car magazines, ran one such contest in the spring of 1956. One of the best designs was from R.H. Gurr who took a Beetle body and turned it into a typical American car of the time with panorama windows, an ornamental B pillar, and a gentle, sloping coupe roof. This new tail fin design was also publicized in Germany, but the discussion surrounding the Gurr Beetle was only found in the press. After all, this car only existed on paper.

At first, Wolfsburg took no notice. But later they became more nervous. In 1957, Alexander Spoerl, author of the bestseller *Mit dem Auto auf du* (*You and Your Car*), wrote in the *Stern* (a leading German magazine) that the Beetle was outdated. Nordhoff immediately sent the VW legal department into action. They came to the conclusion that someone had "commissioned" the article and threatened legal action. Germany's largest magazine for mechanics at the time, *Hobby* (circulation over 400,000), asked provocatively, "Does the VW have to be that way?" and suggested a switch to an all-enveloping body.

VW only began to actively advertise in Germany at the beginning of the 1960s. Prior to this, announcing new sales and production records had seemed to be enough. That changed in August 1962 when Opel introduced the Kadett, the most successful Beetle competitor of all time.

"Fine-sounding speeches only," griped Dieter Korp in *Auto Motor und Sport.* He spoke about the strength of the steel, the possible need for a stronger body and higher costs. Their competition, the monthly magazine *automobil-Technik und Sport* jumped into the discussion in February 1959 with a cutting attack on their Stuttgart colleagues. They said that their competition's article was damaging for the Volkswagen factory (they called it a "disservice") because it made people think that even if VW wanted to build a new body, they couldn't. After this, the discussion calmed down a bit when Nordhoff declared that the Beetle concept would not be changed: "Improvements will continue to be implemented with model changes."

Nordhoff Under Pressure

In the 1960s, the best-known and powerful German boss was visibly coming under more and more pressure, in spite of record sales. In 1962, for example, the trade and commerce minister and vice chancellor at the time, Ludwig Erhard, attempted to get involved in the business politics at Volkswagen.

Erhard had given a radio and television speech (later known as his moderation speech) on March 21, 1962, appealing to the public. "I am turning to the German people at a serious hour. We must take responsibility and act to stop the dangerous developments that are looming on the horizon. We must act quickly to avert disaster." He was reacting to what he saw as excessive union demands. The 1.3 million construction workers wanted a salary increase of 5.2%; public officials were demanding 9%, while the 220,000 organized steelworkers at IG Metall were asking for 10% and an additional week of vacation.

Erhard was even more infuriated when VW announced that as of April 1, the German price for the VW 1200 would be increased DM 240 to DM 4,980. He had just asked everyone to be reasonable, but no one was listening. Not even VW took notice, even though the government was a large stockholder in the factory and a member of

Heinrich Nordhoff: Honorary professor, honorary doctorates from Hamburg, Göttingen and Boston, honorary senator, honorary citizen, Grand Officer of the Italian Order of Merit, Knight of the Order of the Holy Grave, holder of the Grand Cross of the German Order of Merit with Star and Epaulette, a member of innumerable supervisory boards, and so on.

Konrad Adenauer visited the VW factory, Germany's largest taxpayer, on April 22, 1955. Adenauer was at the pinnacle of his power; in October the last of the German prisoners of war returned home from Soviet prison camps.

the supervisory board. So the vice chancellor, who was running the government when Adenauer was on vacation in Italy, increased the pressure on VW—without success. Nordhoff's reacted by saying that he felt it was unfortunate that Professor Erhard's speech "came at the same time as our measure," but he was trying to "ensure the future of the Volkswagen factory." This argument couldn't be denied. The metal workers had negotiated an eventual increase of 10.8%, and Nordhoff was trying to use VW's price increase to make up for a part of these costs. Erhard's answer was a cabinet decision in which they stated they were concerned that VW had not retracted the price increase. When that didn't do anything, the CDU/CSU party demanded (after Erhard's suggestion) that the government reduce import duties for foreign cars starting at the beginning of May. By the middle of the month, the government agreed to reduce the duties. This was against the will of Chancellor Adenauer, who for the first time was not backed by his party.

After 1963, the number of foreign cars registered gradually increased. The biggest winners were Renault, Simca, and Fiat. *Der Spiegel* used the following comparison: 786,024 new cars were registered during the winter season 1965-66 (between October 1965 and March 1966) and imports had an 11.6% market share; during the winter season 1966-67, new registrations had dropped to 629,169 while imports now had 15% of the market. All German car manufacturers suffered: VW's share dropped from 32.4% (1965) to 28.8%, a loss that Nordhoff declared the responsibility of the economic policies of the German government, now under Chancellor Erhard.

In December 1966, the finance minister at the time, Franz-Josef Strauss, had introduced measures to reduce the budget deficit. He reduced the kilometer rate from 25 to 18 pfennigs and increased the oil tax. This increased the cost of a liter (0.26 gallons)

DER SPIEGEL
13. JAHRGANG • Nr. 40
30. SEPTEMBER 1959 • 1 DM
ERSCHEINT MITTWOCHS
VERLAGSORT HAMBURG
NOCH EINE MILLION VOM GLEICHEN TYP
Volkswagen-Generaldirektor Nordhoff (siehe „SPIEGEL-Gespräch")

Left:
At the end of the 1950s, the questions about a successor to the Beetle became more and more penetrating, and not only from the automobile press. Even the newsmagazine *Der Spiegel* had questions (1959). Nevertheless, Nordhoff stuck steadfastly to the rear engine concept.

Below:
Even if the one-model policy did remain for a long time, Wolfsburg engineers built a number of prototypes. Some survived, such as this EA 48, a compact prototype from 1952 with a two-cylinder boxer engine in the front.

of fuel by three pfennigs. At the same time, liability premiums increased by up to 12.5%. Nordhoff expressed his resentment in an interview in *Der Spiegel*: "All plans to stabilize the out-of-control budget are targeted at the automobile industry." He estimated that sales in Germany could plunge up to 30% in the coming year. And drop they did. This meant 42 part-time days at VW, layoffs at Opel, and part-time work at Ford. The number of new cars registered in Germany dropped to the 1950 level. VW alone sold 57,724 cars less than the year before. Nordhoff called for one-year tax free for new cars, which would have saved the Beetle buyer DM 200. The government in Bonn was adamant there would be no subsidies.

The government reacted to Nordhoff's attack on taxes with a harsh critique of VW model strategy from the finance minister, who spoke in front of a group of Bavarian textile company executives in Munich. Their sales crisis was their own fault; if a model's "distinction and comfort" weren't making the model successful, the "name" wasn't going to help. The next morning, the large headline of the newspaper *Bild* read, "VW has been asleep."

VW took the offensive. They opened their archives to three *Der Spiegel* editors to show them what Wolfsburg engineers had been up to in the last two decades in terms of new models and Beetle successors. Since 1952, Nordhoff had ordered more than 70 designs built, only to discard them later. Half of the cars had been destroyed; the rest were stored in corrugated iron vaults. The

EA 160, 1960: the front is a Type 3, the rear a Rover.

EA 266, 1969: This is what the Beetle successor should have looked like. The mid-engine car was developed by Porsche, a project that the future VW chief, Ferdinand Piëch, worked on. After Nordhoff died, Kurt Lotz put a stop to the project, even though several hundred million deutsche marks had already been invested.

A bird's-eye view of the Volkswagen factory in the mid-1960s. On the right is the central canal, in the background, the power plant. The bomb that fell on the power plant luckily didn't explode; otherwise the "miracle of Wolfsburg" would probably never have come to be.

models ranged from a two-cylinder with 0.8-liter displacement to a six-cylinder with 2 liter displacement and 75 DIN hp. There were two-seaters, enlarged Beetles, and models designed by Pininfarina, Ghia and Porsche. Up to DM 200 million had been invested for some. The common theme running throughout was that the engine and transmission were one unit and not water-cooled. The *Der Spiegel* editors explained the lack of go-ahead for any potential successor this way: "The engineers and salespeople felt none of the designs were good enough compared to the Beetle of the century designed by Ferdinand Porsche. The success of the Beetle all over the world, the quality of VW's cars, and the service centers oriented around the Beetle made a decision for a successor incredibly difficult."

Heinrich Nordhoff died April 12, 1968. His successor was Kurt Lotz, whose difficult job it now was to find a Beetle replacement.

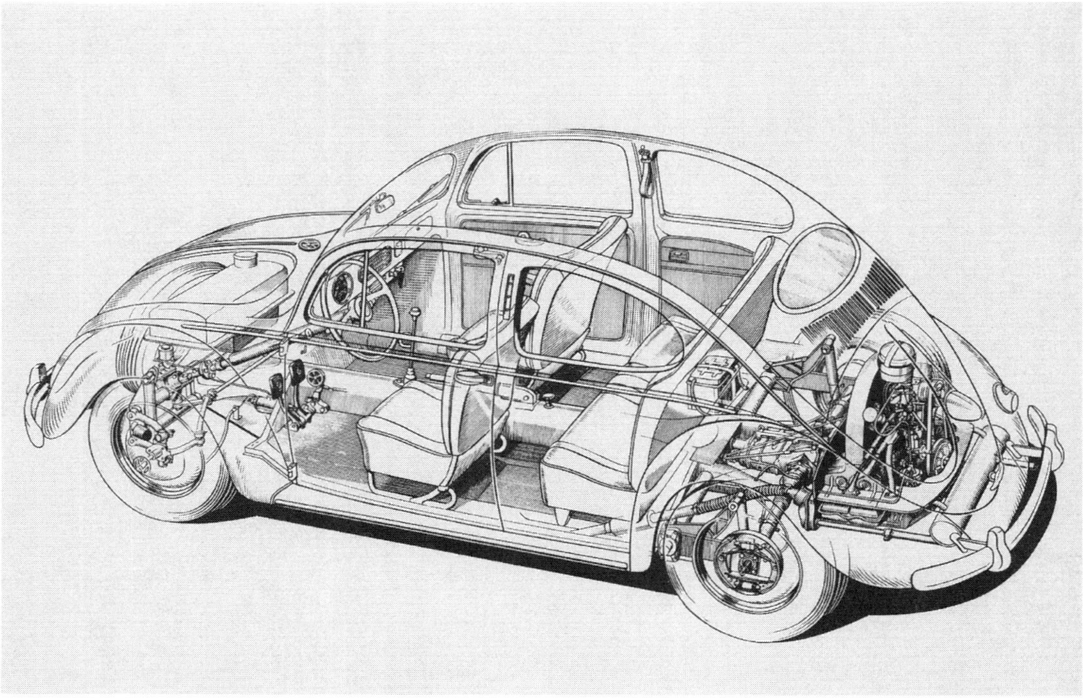

Chapter 2

Type 1 Beetle (1945-85)

Many cars helped shape the history of the automobile: the Ford Model T, the Austin Mini, or even the VW Golf. But the most successful by far was the VW Beetle. Strangely enough, this Volkswagen is the one car among the success stories that couldn't be copied—New Beetle notwithstanding.

The Design

The Body

The Beetle body with its round form was made of sheet steel; the body and fenders were 0.88-mm thick steel, the hood and doors somewhat thinner at 0.75 mm. The hinges of the doors (with stops in the front) were on the outside. That never changed throughout production. Only the driver-side door, with its pull handle outside and rotating handle inside, could be locked from the outside. The passenger-side door could only be locked from the inside. Up to 1949, even the engine cover handle could be locked; this changed in mid-1949. The hood was opened via a bowden cable from the inside. The trunk could hold about 70 liters (2.5 ft^{3}), with the 41-liter (including the 5-liter reserve) fuel tank taking up the rest of the room in the front. The tank's shape and design were changed many times, first to add a ventilation hole and later, to make more room for storage. Gasoline fumes vented into the trunk. There was also a rear trunk, the small 130-liter (4.6 ft^{3}) compartment behind the rear seats.

The 950-mm-wide doors had crank windows. The rear side windows could not be opened. The one-piece windshield was installed at a 30° angle toward the rear. Two windshield wipers took care of keeping the windshield clear during inclement weather. The wipers only returned to a park position at the lower left in the export models.

Left above:
Anatomy of a world champion: Cutaway view from 1953.

Left below:
Beetle puzzle: A Volkswagen was made up of 5000 parts, as this ad from 1965 shows.

The Chassis

Model: Type 51
Built: 1945-46
Engine: 4-cylinder, boxer, air-cooled
Valves: ohv, central camshaft
Displacement: 1131 cm^3
Bore x stroke: 75 x 64 mm
DIN horsepower (kW) @ rpm: 25 (18) @ 3300
Drive: rear wheels
Carburetion: one Solex 26 VFJ
Transmission: 4F, 1R (off-road auxiliary transmission)
Brakes: drums f/r
Top speed: 80 km/h
Curb weight kg: 755
Tires: 5.25-16
Wheelbase: 2400 mm
Track f/r: 1356/1360 mm
L x W x H: 4070 x 1540 x 1630 mm

The Beetle base was a solid (140 mm wide by 165 mm high) tubular backbone frame, wide in the front to accept the front axle and forked in the rear to support the engine. A cross-member with the rear suspension mounts was welded into the fork. The substructure was installed on top of that. The connectors for the accelerator, brake and clutch pedals as well as for the hand brake, shift lever and heating were installed in the oval of the tubular backbone frame.

The front suspension was quite progressive for its time with two trailing links, transverse torsion bars and simple lever-type shock absorbers (double-acting starting in 1949). The axle housing was composed of two cross-members, one above the other. Each contained a leaf spring bundle of five and four springs, respectively. The two trailing links were installed at the end of the leaf springs. They were connected by a bearing bracket. A link pin secured the bearing bracket to the steering knuckle. The bottom of the shock absorbers sat on the lower trailing arms.

In the rear was a dual swing-arm suspension. The drive shafts were located in axle tubes that ran on either side of the transmission housing to the wheels. At the end of each tube was a spring plate connected to a torsion bar made of flat steel supported by a rubber bearing. These transverse torsion bars were surrounded by a protective sleeve. They were mounted at the center on the frame. The ends of the spring plates were free.

Rear shock absorbers were lever-type until April 1951, when double-acting telescopic shock absorbers became standard. Front and rear shocks were of different stroke lengths, 90 mm in the front and 130 mm in the rear. Later, to tell them apart, front shocks were painted black and the rear red.

Braking was via an ATE non-servo drum brake system that acted on all four wheels. The Standard model had mechanical brakes with the required rods and bowden cable installed in the frame. The hand brake lever was located on the frame tunnel.

The Engine

The engine had four cylinders and was air-cooled. It was a four-stroke flat-four design. The engine, clutch, transmission and final drive were all integrated in the same housing. The entire drive unit was located in the frame fork behind the rear axle secured with four bolts. The valves were actuated by push rods and rocker arms. With a 75-mm bore and 64-mm stroke, the engine had a total displacement of 1131 cm^3. The engine produced 25 DIN hp @ 3300 rpm and was cooled by a radial fan. The fan pulley driven by a fan belt sat above the engine on the extended generator shaft. At full power the sixteen blades pumped 450 liters of air per second onto the four

A peek at the engine compartment of a 1949 model with its mushroom-shaped air filter. This style replaced the previous pan-shaped one. On the right of the engine compartment is a convenient holder for replacement spark plugs.

cylinders. The impeller was located in a metal housing; air baffles directed the air. The third cylinder always got a little less air than the others did. That didn't change until the 1971 model year when the Wolfsburg engineers moved the oil cooler.

The flat-four's forced-feed lubrication gear was driven by the camshaft. Oil was fed through a pickup screen located in the crankcase under a cover secured by six bolts. Service requirements stated that the screen was to be cleaned at every oil change. The oil cooler played an important role in the oil circulation within the Beetle's engine. The flat tube cooler was located in the heater air stream, which meant if the cooler was leaking the heater air began to smell. The pressure regulation oil valve didn't circulate all the oil through the cooler until the oil temperature reached 80° C. With a cold engine, the lubricant went right to the lubrication points. The engine was equipped with an oil pressure switch; the dipstick was located on the right side of the engine.

A Solex downdraft carburetor with acceleration pump and butterfly valve supplied the fuel-air mixture to the cylinders via a transverse intake pipe. The intake pipe was surrounded by an aluminum pre-heater. The warm air entered the heater pipe at the right rear exhaust connection flange and then flowed into the left muffler. This was designed to increase mixture evaporation, partic-

ularly on a cold engine. A pan-shaped air filter was installed on top of the carburetor. The shape of the air filter changed many times. An oil-bath air filter was at first only available for certain export countries and Cabriolets. It was later standard in other models. The muffler was installed transversely to the rear of the engine with only one exhaust pipe at first. Power was transferred via a single-plate dry clutch made by Fichtel & Sachs (180 mm diameter). The shift lever was in the center of the car. Only the two upper gears out of the four were synchronized.

Early 34 DIN hp engine with damper heating. Crankcase ventilation went right into the outside air and not, as in later models, into the air filter. (Air filter not installed in this photograph.)

Volkswagen Standard/Export 1945-65

At first the Beetle was available in two versions: Standard and Export sedans. The Export version was also available in Germany as a deluxe version at extra cost.

There were also two Cabriolets, which will be discussed in detail later. The only differences between the Standard and Export cars were in equipment. Handling and performance were identical. In one of the first driving tests, dated summer 1949, Joachim Fischer had the opportunity to put the Beetle through its paces for

Right: Porsche masterpiece, the KdF car from 1938. What Volkswagen called the Type 1, Porsche called the Type 60.

Model: Type 11 Standard
Built: 1946-53
Engine: 4-cylinder, boxer, air-cooled
Valves: ohv, central camshaft
Displacement: 1131 cm^3
Bore x stroke: 75 x 64 mm
DIN horsepower (kW) @ rpm: 25 (18) @ 3300
Drive: rear wheels
Carburetion: one Solex 26 VFJ
Transmission: 4F, 1R
Brakes: drums f/r
Top speed: 105 km/h
Curb weight kg: 720
Tires: 5.00-16 (5.60-15)
Wheelbase: 2400 mm
Track f/r: 1290/1250 mm
L x W x H: 4070 x 1540 x 1630 mm

the Stuttgart-based magazine *Motor Rundschau*. Fischer's report was written in the magazine's standard telegram style.

"Mature four-seater, a small mid-size car, with good balance between performance and fuel economy. One of the most advanced European cars. For its size, fast and lively, excellent performance even on poor roads with many curves. Wheelbase is good for a car with a rear engine, track not yet taken advantage of fully. Road holding: the low, short engine in spite of its location behind the rear axle has almost no negative effect on handling. Solid, even at maximum weight on wet, slippery streets and in corners. With only one to two passengers, recommend you add some weight to the front when driving under slippery conditions (for example, put some luggage or one to two full fuel containers in the front trunk area). Suspension: balanced . . . minimal leaning in curves. Brakes: (new version) for mechanical brakes, balanced and effective. Shifting: short shift lever in the center, easy to shift (exact double declutching required) via the shift rod. Synchronization would help, in spite of this. Interior: comfortable seats, rear seat bench could be a bit longer . . . footwell somewhat reduced due to center tunnel . . . good view including directly in front of the car from all seats . . . engine air-cooling not too noisy, better sound absorbing material would . . . help." At the end of the article, a look at the price

list: In 1948 (after the currency reform), the Standard Beetle cost DM 5300. That year, 8184 Beetles were delivered, almost all of them for official agencies. The Export Beetle was available starting mid-1949 and cost DM 5450.

The first model year where visible changes were made to the Beetle was in 1953. On March 10, 1953, a Type 1 Beetle with the chassis number 1-0454 951 came off the assembly line. This was the first car without the split window, which had become a thing of the past. The new window not only looked more modern but also improved the view to the rear: glass area increased 23%. Part of the increased area was taken over in 1954 by the white text "jetzt um 5 PS stärker" ("now with 5 more horsepower").

In addition, Wolfsburg engineers had completely reworked the original engine designed by Franz Reimspiess. The stroke remained the same, but the bore increased from 75 mm to 77 mm. Total engine displacement was now 1192 cm^3. Together with a compression increase to 6.1, the engine produced 30 DIN hp instead of 25; top speed increased from 102 km/h to 110. In comparison, a Ford Taunus 12 M at the time had 38 DIN hp and could go 115 km/h, while an Opel Rekord had 40 DIN hp and went 120 km/h. These cars, though, were more expensive; a Beetle cost DM 4000 while an Opel cost a much higher DM 5259. When the prices were dropped in 1955 to celebrate the 1 millionth beetle built on August 5, 1955, you could get a Standard Beetle for as little as DM 3790.

In 1955, German car manufacturers built 705,418 passenger cars; 279,986 of those were built by the 31,570 workers at the Wolfsburg factory. VW sales that year were DM 1.41 billion, just behind Daimler-Benz with its DM 1.44 billion. The Stuttgart manufacturer had built 63,683 passenger cars and 30,000 trucks. This made VW the fourth largest passenger car manufacturer, behind General Motors, Ford and Chrysler.

Loading cars in Wolfsburg, 1950. Large VW dealers, such as Hahn in Stuttgart, picked up cars with their own trucks. VW's German market share that year was over 40%, with an average of 342 cars sold each day.

Model year 1949: The export model was introduced on July 1. It cost DM 5450 and could be recognized by the chrome trim. On the inside, the dashboard was different from the Standard Beetle.

1951 models: Vents on the side just to the rear of the front fender. The picture shows the Export model, with its new windshield trim and Wolfsburg coat of arms above the hood handle.

1951 models: VW could have installed turn signals instead of the semaphore indicators as early as 1951. This suggestion came from the VW supplier Bosch. Note also the large headlights as well as the radio antenna in the middle of the windshield.

The Beetle was used as a basis for a number of variants. This picture shows the Beetle ambulance built by Miesen, a car officially incorporated into the VW program. Miesen built 500 of these Type 17 cars up until 1960.

1952 models: The Export model had special door, side and window trim. Tail lights had heart-shaped lenses for the brake lights.

The most important model changes and improvements VW 1200 (1945-65):

1945-48: No visible changes to the body.

1945: May-June, 1785 cars built (by the end of the year) for occupying forces and official agencies.

1946: 10,020 VWs built; purchase by private citizens only possible with ration coupon. Price, RM 5000. Available in gray, blue, and black (RM= reichsmark).

October 14, 10,000th Beetle built.

1947: August, start of export to the Netherlands.

1949: January, double heater control cable.

March, transmission housing made of magnesium alloy; initial oil filling, 2.5 L.

May, trunk cover latch released from the inside, light-colored two-spoke steering wheel (had been black, three-spoke) for Export models. Production start for Export models and Karmann Cabriolet. High-gloss paint, chrome trim.

July, enamel paint instead of nitrocellulose paint.

August, telescopic shock absorbers in the front.

September, tie rod with left- and right-hand thread.

October, larger accelerator pedal roller.

1950: January, front upper and lower five leaf-bundle torsion bar.

April, hydraulic service brake; folding sunroof (made by Golde) available for DM 2 5 0 . Wing windows in the side windows.

May, thermostat added for automatic regulation of cooling air; autothermic pistons.

August, hardened exhaust valves; valve seats made of chromium-nickel steel.

1951: January, crankcase made of magnesium alloy; ventilation flaps on the side.

March, fiber camshaft gear (Export).

April, windshield trim, rear telescopic shock absorbers (Export). Door contact switch for automatic interior lighting. New heating elements.

October, 250,000th car built.

1952: October, upper three gears synchronized (Export models only). Carburetor with accelerator pump. Increased front and rear suspension travel, six-leaf torsion bars, reduced torsion diameter. 15-inch wheels replace 16-inch wheels; tires, 5.60-15 on 4 J x 15 rims. Top speed, 105 km/h, 0-100 km/h in 47.3s. Vents in front quarter pan. Modified bumpers. New dashboard without left storage compartment; glove compartment with cover on right, semaphore indicator switch beneath steering wheel. Oval grill covering horns. Two brake lights including taillights.

1953: March, enlarged rear window, no longer split.

1954: January, 30 DIN hp engine introduced; displacement increased to 1192 cm^3, compression ratio 6.1:1. Oil-bath air filter, enlarged intake valves. Different gearing for Export model. Front track Export model 1305 mm, for Standard 1290 mm. Top speed, 110 km/h, 0-100 km/h in 47s.

August, compression increased to 6.6, 160-watt generator.

1955: August, single-chamber muffler with double exhaust, PVC sunroof, new brake lights and taillights installed higher on the rear fenders. Larger trunk space due to redesigned shape of fuel tank.

1956: August, tubeless tires; better engine compartment; more powerful starter; stronger windshield wiper motor.

1957: August, windshield and rear window area increased significantly; new shape of rear engine cover; license plate lighting with pan-shaped lens. New dashboard.

1958: August, large side mirror.

1959: August, fixed door handle with push button. Two-spoke steering wheel with sunken center; with a horn ring for Export models. Openings beneath the rear seat covered by heel plates. Footrest for passenger; automatic return for semaphore indicators. Better handling due to lowering swing-arm axle pivot.

1960: July, end of production of 30 DIN hp Export Beetle.

August, introduction of new Export Beetle with 34 DIN hp and fully synchronized transmission (VW 1200). Compression 7.0, rated speed 3600rpm, modified valve timing. Max. torque, 8.4 mkg. Top speed: 115 km/h, 0-100 km/h in 33s. Automatic choke, hydraulic steering dampers, modified transmission ratios. DM 4600. Standard and Export, flatter fuel tank with ventilation to the outside; trunk volume increased by 65%. Windshield washer; asymmetric low beams. Turn signals replace semaphore indicators; pre-heated air filter.

1961: August, only Export, cam-and-roller steering; two-chamber taillights. Mechanical fuel gauge. Ignition and steering lock. Door stays. Pneumatic windshield washers.

1962: April, hydraulic service brake now in Standard model. Fresh-air heating with heat exchanger.

August, improved valve train; better footwell insulation.

1963: August, wider license plate lights. Steel crank sunroof instead of the folding sunroof. Horn buttons in steering spokes. Door handles made of chrome-plated stainless steel.

December, enlarged front turn signals. Modified generator.

1964: January, wax-based underbody coating.

August, two heating levers replace rotary knob. Heat exchanger with warm-air outlet increased by 60 mm. Cooling air now regulated by four dampers within the housing instead of via throttle valve. Window area increased by 15%, larger rear window. Belt line lowered by 3 cm. New wiper arms, locking handle for wing windows (used to be push button); sun visors can be swung to the side. Foldable rear seat, rear leg room increased by 20 mm. Outer mirrors 20 mm larger.
November, standard Beetle becomes the 1200A (engine remains the same). VW1200 Export gets fully synchronized transmission.

1965: July, production of 1200A with 30 DIN hp engine ends. The new VW1200A has 34 DIN hp.

1954 models: The Volkswagen no longer had the split rear window, but it did come with the 30 DIN hp engine.

1955 models: 279,986 Volkswagens came off the assembly line that year, including the one millionth Volkswagen on August 5. To celebrate that day, Heinrich Nordhoff dropped prices: 3790 marks for a standard Beetle, 4600 for the export model.

1957 models: A luggage puzzle when loading the trunk. Although the shape of the gas tank had been redesigned many times (the last time in 1955), it was still difficult to load the trunk: it didn't hold more than 85 liters.

1957 models: After the factory vacation in August, the Beetle got a completely new dashboard, including a wider glove compartment. The speedometer was the only thing that stayed the same. The special trim was a sign of an Export model.

Three Beetle generations: On the left, a 1303 with its characteristic elephant-feet lights; in the center, a VW 1200 (model year 1960) with retrofitted back-up lights (a typical accessory at the time); and on the right, a VW 1300 from 1965 with two-chamber lights.

1961 models: 34 DIN hp engine and turn signals instead of semaphore indicators, both for the Export (photo) and the standard Beetle. Only government offices tended to be interested in the plain Standard Beetle; of the 725,939 1960 Beetles, only 3.4% were Standard.

Model year 1963: Many small improvements, including fresh-air heating. This model is easily identified by the solid trim piece on the hood, without the Wolfsburg coat of arms.

VW 1200 (1960-85)

Model: VW 1200
Built: 1960-65
Engine: 4-cylinder, boxer, air-cooled
Valves: ohv, central camshaft
Displacement: 1192 cm3
Bore x stroke: 77 x 64 mm
DIN horsepower (kW) @ rpm: 34 (25) @ 3600
Drive: rear wheels
Carburetion: one Solex 28 PICT-1
Transmission: 4F, 1R
Brakes: drums, f/r
Top speed: 112 km/h
Curb weight: 730 kg
Tires: 5.60-15
Wheelbase: 2400 mm
Track f/r: 1305/1250 mm
L x W x H: 4070 x 1540 x 1500 mm

In the 1960s, because VW ads didn't really have anything completely new to talk about, the continual model improvements became more and more important as advertising material. When VW introduced the 1961 model year with its numerous improvements after the factory vacation in August, this was the first model year whose advantages were strongly emphasized this time successfully in ads and brochures. By the end of the year, large numbers of people were again visiting the now 1300 VW showrooms.

The car for this model year looked like the old one only at first glance. From the perspective of VW, however, a lot had been done to the car. Easily recognized were the new turn signals on the fenders that replaced the semaphore indicators on the B pillar. The engine was modified as well: it was the one that had been installed in the vans built in Hanover-Stöcken since May 1956. In the bus, the engine only produced 30 DIN hp, but in the version of the engine first installed only in the Export Beetle, 34 DIN hp were available at 3600 rpm. The flat-four engine looked like its predecessor, but it actually had been modified in almost every aspect. A new air filter was installed, and the biggest change was the introduction of a three-piece engine block with one-piece transmission housing. The distance between the cylinders was now 10 mm, something that improved engine cooling. The use of a stronger crankshaft with different bearings made the flat-four more reliable. The valve gear, the shape of the combustion chamber, the valve diameter and the camshaft were also modified. Compression rose from 6.6 to 7.0. A new Solex carburetor with automatic choke was installed. Due to the modified shape of the fuel tank, trunk capacity rose from 85 liters to 140 liters.

Model year 1961: Since 1956, the Beetle had been the only car on the German market that still came with semaphore indicators. That changed after the factory vacation in 1960.

Starting in August 1964: larger windows, windshield wipers parked on the left and engine compartment cover with push-button latch.

Fresh-air heating was standard equipment beginning in December 1962. The heated air, which before had been warmed by the hot cylinders, now flowed through a heat exchanger. The new system worked pretty well, even if the heated air still smelled like exhaust (as before) when the system rusted through enough to allow exhaust gases into the interior. The Beetle retained the two big air hoses in the engine compartment throughout its life.

Model year 1965: 15% larger glass area, windshield extended higher into the roof, larger side windows.

All four gears were now synchronized. This long-needed improvement sent the advertising department into euphoria with

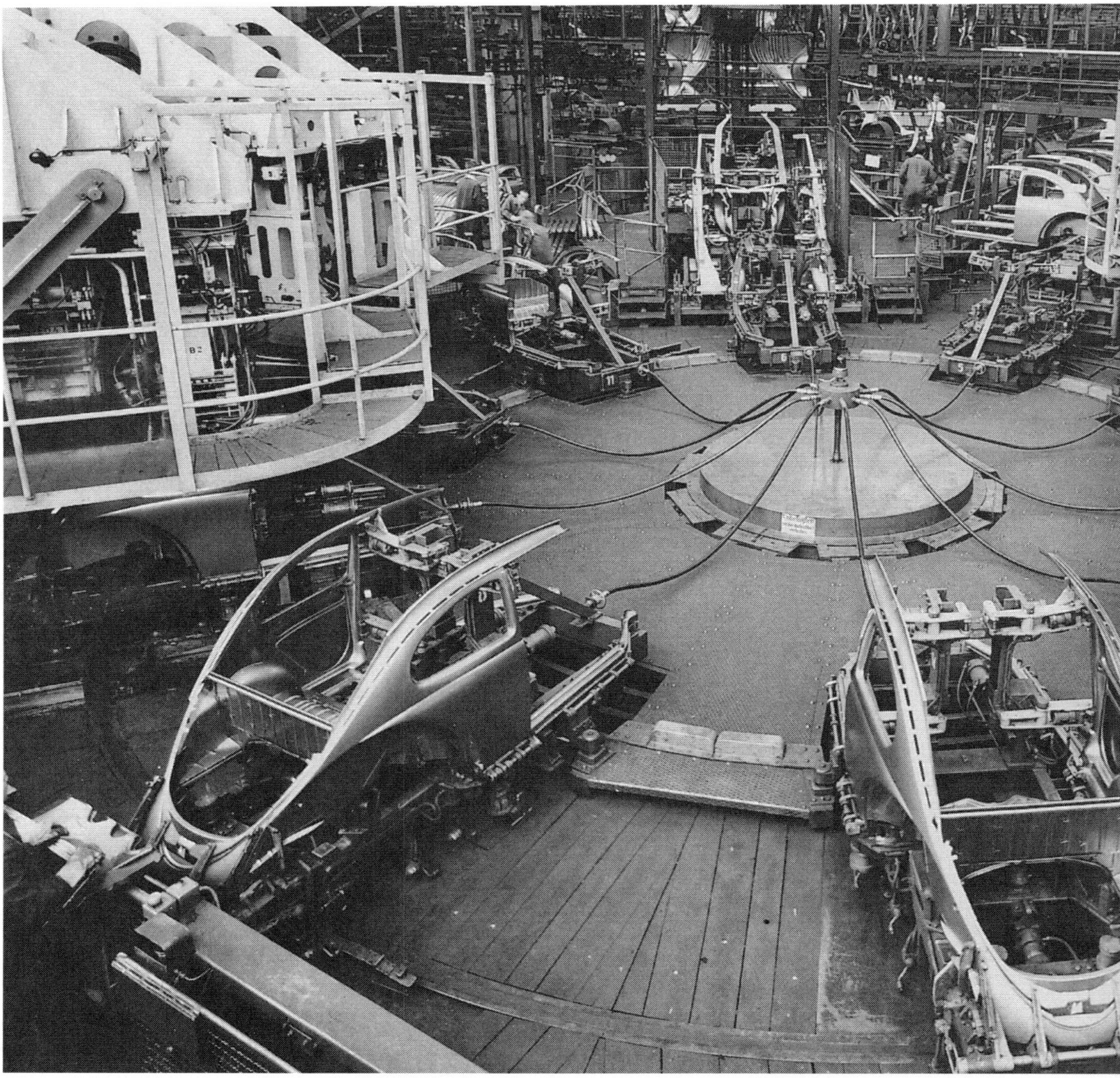

their slogan for the new model year (the last one that used drawings by the VW advertiser Ernst Reuters) "Das Automobil des vernünftigen Fortschritts" (The car of sensible progress).

All in all, VW listed 30 improvements, which included the technical changes noted above as well as improvements for the car's occupants. These included a passenger-side grab handle, a second sun visor, asymmetric low beams, and a speedometer that went up to 140 km/h. The last change was really not needed; the Export Beetle could only go 115 km/h. "With the 140 km/h speedometer, people who drive fast will no longer have to experience a pinned needle," according to Reinhard Seiffert from *Auto, Motor und Sport*. As the magazine *Motor Rundschau* confirmed, DM 4600 for a 34

Circular assembly line: A similar system was also used for the front of the Beetle. This one had eight stations and was able to handle up to 240 bodies-in-white.

DIN hp Export Beetle was a good investment: "The 1961 Beetle has 34 DIN hp. If you haven't seen the new car, it's worth a thorough look . . . look at everything, every corner, every angle and you will come to the conclusion that there are very few automobiles designed and built with such care. Because the original VW design was so progressive back then, the new 1961 model . . . is basically the old car, but still one of the most progressive cars."

Three years and numerous minor changes later, people seemed to be growing tired of the Beetle. This was at least the case for automobile journalists. "Writing a test report for the VW 1200 is a fairly monotonous task. Basically nothing has changed since 1960 when the last major changes were made to the engine, suspension and chassis," complained *Auto, Motor und Sport* in Issue 19/1964. They continued, "It may be notable for Volkswagen that they have improved the heating and enlarged the windows, but let's face it, there are cars in the same price range that have had even better heating and even larger windows since day one."

Reinhard Seiffert, who three years earlier had been completely satisfied with the Beetle, didn't really have anything good to say this time, "The Beetle needs to have at least 40 DIN hp to not be a road hazard . . . the slowest on the road dictates the speed (on the highways) and the slowest today just happens to be a car of which too many have been sold, the VW . . . the VW is in no way able to keep up with the improvements in road handling and comfort made today."

The original Standard Beetle was only available until November 1964, then it became the VW 1200A. A year later, this model got the 34 DIN hp engine. The difference between Export and Standard models disappeared from the sales brochures. The base car, the

Model year 1964: This car now boasted a steel crank sunroof instead of the folding sliding sunroof used in the Export model, larger turn signals on the front fenders, and a new license plate light.

Model year 1965: The press and customers had been asking for it for a long time and it was now available: the rear seat-back could finally be completely folded down. The luggage area, 1 m long and 1.25 m wide, was carpeted.

Model: VW 1200 A
Built: 1964-66
Engine: 4-cylinder, boxer
Valves: ohv, central camshaft
Displacement: 1192 cm^3
Bore x stroke: 77 x 64 mm
DIN horsepower (kW) @ rpm: 30 (22) @ 3400
Drive: rear wheels
Carburetion: one Solex 28 PICT-1
Transmission: 4F, 1R
Brakes: drums, f/r
Top speed: 115 km/h
Curb weight kg: 750
Tires: 5.60-15
Wheelbase: 2400 mm
Track f/r: 1305/1288 mm
L x W x H: 4070 x 1540 x 1500 mm

During the mid-1960s an average of 4550 Beetles were built each day. An assembly line was even installed at Auto Union in Ingolstadt. This photograph, though, is of the paint shop at Wolfsburg.

Left: Model year 1967: Only small interior modifications were made including the large, black dashboard knobs made of soft plastic. This improved safety for vehicle occupants.

1200A, had the chassis from the VW 1300 and cost DM 4290. The VW 1300 took over from the previous Export Beetle. The 1200A didn't last very long. It was removed from the model line in August 1966 and returned in the spring of 1967. When it returned it didn't get any of the improvements made during the new model year. It also had to wait for the dual-circuit brake system the faster Beetle had received. But the car known as the "NSKK" (Nordhoff's Striptease-Krisen-Käfer—Nordhoff's striptease crisis Beetle) as a joke was actually a very good buy at DM 4485 and well loved.

The run on the new basic Beetle helped to make up for the 20% fewer sales after the last price increase (prices went up twice in 1968). In 1968, 61,833 VW 1200s were sold in Germany; in 1969, this was 77,209. Most of the cars were sold to official agencies. Private customers favored the 1300; 164,681 were sold in 1968 and 204,445 in 1969.

The basic Beetle was also at the low end of the VW price list during the 1970s. During 1974 and 1975, it was built in the bus factory in Hanover. The VW 1200 at DM 4695 was one of the least-expensive cars on the German market at the time. Citroën's 2CV, an aged design as well but much less powerful at 23 or 25 DIN hp, started at DM 4200. The Fiat 500 also cost a few hundred deutsche marks less. But neither of the imports could match the image of the Beetle. What they did have on the Beetle was their better standard equipment. The least expensive Beetle included only what was absolutely necessary: simple bumpers, oval taillights, no air vents in the front trunk cover or rear engine cover, black window frames, black exhaust pipes, and a lack of chrome (there wasn't even a model insignia) made the 1200 a "gray mouse." The interior also showed signs of having come under the red pen; there was a two-spoke black steering wheel, a reserve handle instead of a fuel gauge, poorly laid rubber mats, no armrest, no grab handles, and the seatbacks were not secured against accidentally tilting forward. Everywhere you looked you saw basic utility. The engine in the rear with 34 DIN hp was poorly insulated. For DM 100 more you could get the 1.3-liter engine with 44 DIN hp. This price also included equalizing springs for the rear axle.

After the 1300 models were phased out, the base Beetle got a 1.2-liter 34 DIN hp or, at extra cost, the 50 DIN hp 1.6-liter engine

Model year 1974: To increase the attractiveness of the Beetle, several special editions were introduced, including the yellow Jeans Beetle. It cost DM 5995 marks and was DM 345 more expensive than the VW 1200 with standard equipment. They both had the same engine.

along with a 12-volt electrical system. Both versions could also be ordered with the L option. With this option, the 1.6-liter Beetle got the rear of the 1303. Nothing had been changed on the chassis with trailing link front axle and rear swing axle. The 50 DIN hp Beetle with the L package came with the equalizing springs on the rear axle and disc brakes in the front. The 1977 1200L cost DM 8470, whereas a base Beetle with 34 DIN hp started at DM 7480. In comparison, a base VW Golf (two doors, 50 DIN hp) started at DM 9195, the top Golf, the GLS (two doors, 75 DIN hp) cost DM 11,420.

The Mexican Beetle

The last Beetle left the assembly line in Emden in January 1978. By that time, a total of 16,255,500 Beetles had been built in the three German factories. Any Beetles that were delivered to showrooms after that came from Mexico. On December 15, 1977, the first Puebla-built Beetles came off the boat in Emden. The Mexican Beetle cost DM 8145 and came with only one engine choice, the 34 DIN hp. All of these Beetles came with the L option, which included chrome bumpers, the elephant foot-shaped taillights, a padded dashboard, adjustable headrests, and three-point automatic seatbelts. The car also had forced ventilation, but not the two-stage fresh-air fan. The rear window was smaller and was actually the same window used between 1965 and 1971. The Mexican Beetle was also equipped with radial tires, chrome trim, a fuel gauge, and a heated rear window.

Six years after the last Beetle was imported to Germany in 1985, the Mexican Beetle got a 1.6-liter engine. As the 1992 Beetle now came with Digifant fuel injection and regulated catalytic converter, independent importers tried their luck. Four DIN hp were lost with the installation of the catalytic converter, but it didn't affect driving characteristics: "When you first get in the car, you immediately notice how vertical the seating position is, like sitting on a kitchen chair . . . shifting is as wobbly as it ever was. There is no power steering . . . is it me or were the last Wolfsburg Beetles quieter? The four-speed transmission is like one in a Porsche in my grandfather's time: the first three gears are relatively low, the fourth on the other hand, incredibly high. Thanks to the large amount of torque, the fourth gear can be used between 60 km/h and the top speed. OK, the 'top' speed is 127 km/h. You can drive at that speed only for a short time, though, otherwise your ears fall off." (Gernot Röthig in the magazine *Auto Zeitung*, issue 24/95).

At the end of 1995, the Rewe retail group offered 300 Beetles in red, blue, black and red, for DM 16,666, as part of their "economic wonder weeks." The cars were quite well equipped: regulated catalytic converter, alarm system, fire extinguisher, interval wipers, reclining seats, a foldable rear seatback, H4 lights,

Model: VW 1200L
Built: 1975-78
Engine: 4-cylinder, boxer
Valves: ohv, central camshaft
Displacement: 1192 cm^3
Bore x stroke: 77 x 64 mm
DIN horsepower (kW) @ rpm: 34 (25) @ 3800
Drive: rear wheels
Carburetion: one Solex 30 PICT-1
Transmission: 4F, 1R
Brakes: drums, f/r
Top speed: 127 km/h
Curb weight: 820 kg
Tires: 5.60-15
Wheelbase: 2400 mm
Track f/r: 1308/1349 mm
L x W x H: 4090 x 1550 x 1500 mm

Beetle production ended in Germany on January 19, 1978, but continued elsewhere, in Puebla at the Mexican VW factory — from some perspectives this was a clear step backwards.

and rear fog light. Volkswagen warned people against buying the cars and explained that spare parts might be difficult to find. The discount store was sued for its one-year guarantee without a mileage limit by the "Zentralvereinigung des Kfz-Gewerbes zur Aufrechterhaltung lauteren Wettbewerbs" (umbrella organization of the automobile trade for maintaining honorable competition). The organization was able to get a temporary injunction, but nobody it no longer mattered: the Beetle promotion had just ended (end of November) and the cars were already sold. The success of that promotion got others interested in the same thing. The largest VW dealer in Munich, for instance, imported 100 Beetles and offered them at DM 15,900. At one dealer in Ratingen (North Rhine-Westfalia), the car cost DM 15,555; an independent dealer in Stuttgart went one further, selling the cars for DM 14,990 in January 1997. You couldn't get a brand new classic car much cheaper than that.

VW 1300 (1965-1973)

In issue 18/1965 of *Auto, Motor und Sport*, Reinhard Seiffert once again took another look at the Volkswagen phenomenon. This time, his conclusion was surprisingly positive. The VW with the largest engine

The Mexican Beetle: The old front end, with the rear of the 1303; this is what the Beetle looks like as it moves toward the next millennium. Sale of the Beetle in Germany ended in 1985.

1981 special edition: The 20 millionth Beetle was built on May 15, 1981, reason enough for the Silver Bug, a silver Beetle with black pinstripes. This special edition cost DM 9380.

1983 special edition: Volkswagen introduced a number of different special editions to combat the staleness of the Beetle. The Special Bug was offered in Mars Red or Black Metallic with gold pinstripes. The special package included a radio and partial leather seats, all for DM 10,045.

1984 special edition: The seats in the Red Velvet Beetle were red velour and blue leatherette.

One of many: Police, fire department, post office, army; the cheapest car built in Germany was an important part of many institutions and clubs. Even the ADAC (German AAA) had VWs.

Say good-bye: The Pewter Gray VW 1200 special edition called "50 years of the Beetle" was the final farewell of the Type 1. The last of the 3000 jubilee Beetles cost DM 11,950. The official send-off took place on October 17, 1985, in Wolfsburg in front of 500 invited guests.

The most important model changes and improvements VW 1200:

1960-65	Changes same as the VW Standard/Export, plus the following:
1960:	August, introduction of VW 1200 with 34 DIN hp; displacement 1192 cm³; compression, 7.0. Automatic choke instead of the cable-controlled flap; improvements in interior equipment (windshield washers, passenger-side grab handle, rotory switch for windshield wipers and washers for Export); tank ventilation to the outside.
1961:	July, steering ratio 14.15:1 (previously 14.34:1).
1962:	April, hydraulic brake actuation, previously via cable. Plastic headliner.
1964:	January, a VW 1200 with an Oettinger-tuned 1300 cm³ and 50 DIN hp engine wins the GT class (up to 1300 cc); driver: Wallrabenstein.
	June, exhaust valve clearance increased by 0.1 mm.
	October, check valve is installed between fuel pump and carburetor.
1965:	August, VW 1200 (Export) replaced by VW 1300. VW 1200A gets the 34 DIN hp engine and uses the same chassis as before. VW 1200 Export, stabilizer, cam-and-roller steering, and steering dampers. Front axle from the VW 1300, ventilated wheel rims with holes. Track, camber and toe-in as in the VW 1300.
	November, VW 1300 clutch now also used in the VW 1200A.
1966:	July, VW 1200A dropped.
1967:	January, reintroduction of the VW 1200 (without the "A," with the 34 DIN hp from the base Beetle). Chassis and body from the VW 1300 but with simplified equipment and less chrome (window frames without trim), no equalizer springs on the rear axle.
	August, safety steering column, vertical headlights, new quarter vent lock, three-point anchoring for seatbelts. Shift lever shortened and moved back, rotary knob for glove compartment. Four-bolt wheels.
1968:	August, diagnostic system introduced. Closed crankcase ventilation system. Modified center speedometer/gauge. Hazard lights standard. Front hood released via lever in glove compartment.
1969:	August, pre-warmed intake air regulated by thermostat. Dual-circuit brake system. Optional, 1300 engine with disc brakes and automatic also available for the VW 1200.
1970:	August, low and high beams only on if ignition switched on. Front and rear towing lugs. Modified ignition lock. Modified control knobs, car jack under rear seat.
1971:	January, automatic turn signals.
	August, larger rear window, rear shelf.
1972:	February, standard front seatback lock.
	August, more stable seat anchoring.
1973:	February, new piston shape; compression ratio, 7.3:1.

August, introduction of taillights and box-shaped bumper in matte black from the 1303. Introduction of VW 1200L with improved option level: chrome bumpers, two-speed windshield wipers with automatic park, and reverse lights at a cost of DM 300. Optional 44 DIN hp engine. Special edition, "Jeans Beetle": Tunis Yellow, pinstripes,seats in jean material, black trim, safety belts, radio, sport wheels 4.5J x 15, heated rear window, fuel gauge, passenger grab handle, rear sun visor, and 12-volt electrical system; DM 5995.

1974: August, VW 1200 without hubcaps or glove compartment cover; simpler door and side trim; front turn signals integrated in bumpers. DM 6395. VW 1200L with improved insulation, trim strips around windows, and lockable glove compartment. Padded dashboard and forced ventilation. Available with 34 or 44 DIN hp engine.

1975: May, 1.3-liter engine with 44 DIN hp dropped.

August, 12-volt electrical system now standard. New model, VW 1200 with 1.6-liter from the 1303 (DM 7920). All 34 DIN hp base Beetles (DM 6995) now have paper air filter. VW 1200L gets two-stage electrical fresh-air fan, four-spoke steering wheel, and door contact switch on the right; 1200L/50 DIN hp (8645) with 03 engine cover and standard rear equalizer springs and front disc brakes.

Optional M package: fuel gauge, rear window defroster, day/night rearview mirror, passenger sun visor, and grab handle.

1976: August, sockets for adjustable headrests; automatic dropped. Prices: DM 7480/8010 and 7940/8470 (1200L/34 DIN hp, and 1200L/50 DIN hp).

1977: August, central diagnostic test circuitry dropped.

1978: January 19, the last German-built Beetle comes off the assembly line in Emden. VW 1200 with 50 DIN hp dropped, only L Beetle with 34 DIN hp available. New VW 1200L built in Puebla, Mexico: DC generator, rear equalizer springs, chrome bumpers without rubber trim, safety glass windshield, rear window defroster, fuel gauge, leather-grain steering wheel, driver- and passenger-side sun visors and grab handles. Smaller rear window. Following dropped from previous L option: two-stage fresh-air fan, and rear shelf. DM 8145.

1979: March, six-year rust-through warranty. DM 8506.

1980: Price increased to DM 9025.

1981: January, new turn signal/wiper switch, electric windshield washer pump (installed in some cars) instead of pneumatic system. 155 SR 15 radial tires, instead of 5.60-15 bias tires.

May, special edition "Silver Bug" (reason: the 20 millionth Beetle built on May 15, 1981). Equipped with silver metallic paint and pinstripes. Stylish seat covers. Radio. Celebratory insignia. DM 9380.

July, ventilation slits on engine cover dropped. Price, DM 9435.

December, DM 9655.

1982: May, electrical windshield washer pump for all models. Introduction of "Jeans Bug" in Alpine White or Mars Red. Pinstripes, all chrome trim now anodized black. Radio, jeans seat covers, door and side trim in blue leatherette, different shift knob. DM 9995.

September, special edition "Special Bug" in Mars Red or Black Metallic. Trim anodized black, gold pinstripes, front and rear insignia, leather/cloth seats, and radio, DM 10,045.

1983: March, three year warranty on paint.

Special edition "Eggplant Beetle": Appropriately colored body and wheels; seats, door and side trim in same color; chrome bumpers, and radio. 3300 built, DM 9480.

Special edition "Ice Blue Metallic Beetle", black-silver pinstripes, blue-gray interior. 200 built, DM 9760.

Special edition "Alpine White", pinstripes, blue-gray interior, no radio, DM 9480.

1984: February, special edition "Ice Blue Metallic Beetle." Equipped same as previous year, DM 9990.

Special edition "Sunny Bug," pinstripes, corduroy seats.

July, special edition "Red Velvet Beetle," pinstripes, interior in red-blue velour (seats) and blue leatherette (side trim); no radio. DM 9990.

September, "Red Velvet Beetle" price raised to DM 10,175.

1985: August, the final 3150 imported from factory arrive at dealers, Tin-Gray Metallic, tinted windows, four-spoke steering wheel, radio, seats with double black/red stripes, sport steel wheels, jubilee plate: "50 Jahre Käfer" (50 years of the Beetle) on the engine cover; 165 SR 15 wheels. DM 11,950.

The Volkswagen with the 1.3-liter engine was sold between 1965 and 1973. The picture shows a VW 1300 built in 1971. This can be recognized by the engine cover (from the 1302) and the air extraction vents in the rear (just behind the quarter window).

Model: VW 1300
Built: 1965-67
Engine: 4-cylinder, boxer
Valves: ohv, central camshaft
Displacement: 1285 cm^3
Bore x stroke: 77 x 69 mm
DIN horsepower (kW) @ rpm:
40 (29) @ 4000
Drive: rear wheels
Carburetion:
one Solex 30 PICT-1
Transmission: 4F, 1R
Brakes: drums, f/r
Top speed: 122 km/h
Curb weight kg: 780
Tires: 5.60-15
Wheelbase: 2400 mm
Track f/r: 1305/1300 mm
L x W x H:
4070 x 1540 x 1500 mm

ever, a 1.3-liter, had woken up and was alive again. This put a damper on some critics who had foreseen the end of the Beetle. This new Beetle had more horsepower and included numerous improvements.

The VW 1300 with its 40 DIN hp was offered from the 1966 model year and put the original Standard Beetle in its place, "Wherever a VW 1300 appeared in August 1965, people turned their heads and stared at the new model as if it was a rare animal. Besides the 1300 on the engine cover and a somewhat different interior, one really couldn't see any difference between this car and millions of other Volkswagens," said Seiffert. This is true: the only visual differences were the insignia and the new open steel wheels with flat hubcaps. The 1300, which took over from the Export Beetle, was not a new design; the increased displacement was due to the new crankshaft taken from the 1500 (Type 3). Maximum engine output rose to 40 DIN hp at 4000 rpm; the compression ratio rose to 7.3, but the Beetle could still be run on regular gasoline. A total of 23 changes differentiated this Beetle from the 1200A. This included a new front axle with ball joints instead of the maintenance intensive link pin. The distance between the cross tubes increased as well. These changes still didn't make the Beetle a truly modern car, but they did make it a better car, something even the critics had to admit. "This is most likely due to the fact that the car holds its value so well. The increase in performance, at only a slight increase in cost, will give buyers impetus as well."

As in the VW 1500, the VW 1300 enjoyed the many changes made due to the dictates of the American market. In 1969 you could get a VW 1300 with 40 DIN hp and front disc brakes (at extra cost) as well as a 1300 with the 1200 engine and front discs, or in combination with the L package.

Both the VW 1200 and VW 1300 were around for the new Beetle generation with the suspension strut front axle. A 1971 VW 1300 cost DM 5495. Besides the required model changes, the car was completely unchanged. This car still came with the old body and the old chassis but was much better equipped inside and out. The 1300 had a chrome insignia on the engine cover to differentiate it from the base Beetle. The former also came with additional air inlets (2 x 5) to be able to adequately cool the more powerful 1.3-liter power plant (44 DIN hp). The equipment installed in the 1300S was the same as the new Super Beetle, the 1302. Both cars were available with the L option, at extra cost. This package now came with a two-stage fresh-air fan (very useful), carpeting, two reverse lights, a padded dashboard, dual-circuit brake system, as well as a day/night rearview mirror and a door pocket on the right. The L option was standard for US Beetles. The car weighed 820 kg and, according to the factory, could go up to 125 km/h (during tests, up to 130 km/h). The 1200 had 10 DIN hp less and its top speed was 115 km/h (curb weight for the 1200 was 760 kg). The VW 1300 was also available with the 34 DIN hp engine. For the 1972 model year, all models came with a four cm taller windshield. Inside there was a new steering wheel with crash pad. A diagnostic connector was installed in the engine compartment. This was due to the new diagnostic computer (developed along with Siemens) VW was introducing in VW shops. The electronic mechanic checked 25 out of the 88 points on the VW maintenance checklist. Each dealer leased a computer for DM 300 a month, much cheaper than human employees. At the end, the VW 1300 cost DM 6330 and disappeared from the model line in August 1973.

VW 1500 (1966-70)

In August 1966, a year after the presentation of the VW 1300, VW started building a Beetle with the 1.5-liter (44 DIN hp) engine from the bus. The only change the VW engineers made to the engine for use in the top-of-the-line Beetle was to enlarge the belt pulley. The increased output (44 DIN hp @ 4000 rpm) was due to a longer stroke, higher compression, and a different carburetor. Top speed rose to 130 km/h, with 0-100 km/h in 22.5 s. This was about twice as fast as a 1300 and ten seconds faster than a VW 1200.

The 44 DIN hp flat-four was known as the most agreeable Beetle power plant ever. Beetles with this engine (except for those

Model: VW 1500
Built: 1966-67
Engine: 4-cylinder, boxer
Valves: ohv, central camshaft
Displacement: 1493 cm^3
Bore x stroke: 83 x 69 mm
DIN horsepower (kW) @ rpm: 44 (32) @ 4000
Drive: rear wheels
Carburetion: one Solex 30 PICT-1
Transmission: 4F, 1R
Brakes: drums, f/r
Top speed: 128 km/h
Curb weight kg: 800
Tires: 5.60-15
Wheelbase: 2400 mm
Track f/r: 1305/1358 mm
L x W x H: 4070 x 1540 x 1500 mm

The most important model changes and improvements VW 1300:

1965-73 Changes same as the VW 1200, plus the following:

1965: August, replaces the VW 1200 Export. Changes include 40 DIN hp engine (1285 cm^3 displacement) and front axle design (cross-tubes further apart, outer trailing links with needle bearings, connected to steering knuckles via ball joints, and 10-leaf torsion bars). DM 4980.

1966: August, introduction of VW 1300A, replaces VW 1200A. Same as the VW 1300, with simpler interior, but with the 40 DIN hp engine. Rear equalizer springs, wider rear track. Changes to engine cover, new door handles, new control knobs and window cranks.

1967: August, fresh-air intake in front of windshield; 12-volt electrical system; dual-circuit brake system; stronger bumpers. Door locks on both sides, tank filler cap outside, two-speed windshield wipers with longer wiper blades, fresh-air ventilation.

1968: August, VW 1300 also available with automatic. Front disc brakes available as an option.

1970: August, new safety steering wheel with crash pad. Rear trunk area with cover that flips up. Engine cover with 26 air inlets. Improved pre-warming of intake. Additional fresh-air outlets on dashboard.

1971: August, engine cover without water collector.

1972: March, 4.5 J x 15 wheels.

August, introduction of VW 1300S: 1.6-liter engine, disc brakes. Optional packages: "M" and "inclement weather package."

October, 44 DIN hp engine with different carburetor, paper air filter instead of oil-bath filter.

1973: July, model line discontinued, replaced by VW 1303A.

cars built for the US) came with standard disc brakes; the switch from drums to disc brakes was possible due to the ball joint front axle. The rear brakes remained drums. The transmission remained the same until the end of the decade; VW installed the well-known four-speed manual transmission, which until 1965 was only fully synchronized in the Export and Cabriolet models.

For model year 1968, due to pressure from the US market, VW introduced a three-speed auto-stick transmission. The auto-stick had a torque converter (only available with the 1500 engine); it worked like a normal transmission, except there was no clutch. Thanks to the torque converter, the Beetle could drive off in any gear. Few Europeans ordered this option, although they would have enjoyed the more complex semi-trailing link rear suspension that came with the auto-stick. The magazine *Motor Rundschau* tested one of these models in their 23/1967 issue, "Easy to start when cold, engine runs well in every situation. Accelerates easily without

any flat spots. Excellent shifting (except for reverse gear). Torque converter and engine are well matched. Excellent road holding for a rear engine car. Very good rear axle with even tracking and camber. Easy to keep car going straight ahead even in crosswinds."

The cars with manual transmission were also very different from their predecessors. American safety regulations, the reason for the facelift, went into effect January 1, 1968. They required not only larger and easier to see taillights, but also many other finishing touches, such as to the door handles. The door opening mechanism was now part of the door handle, which meant the pushbutton, which had just been introduced a year earlier, was dropped. This was designed to prevent the door from opening unintentionally in the case of a rollover. The regulations also required the use of flatter and softer knobs on the dashboard, a 12-volt electrical system, vertical headlights, stronger and higher bumpers as well as mounting points for retrofitting seatbelts. A padded dashboard, hazard lights, front seats with integrated head-rests, reverse lights, brake warning light, and a rear window defroster were standard for US models, whereas these cost DM 200 more for buyers in Germany. Some models bound for other European countries also had varying equipment levels. A dual-circuit brake system was also used.

Beetle for the social climber: For the 1967 model year, VW introduced the VW 1500 with a 1.5-liter engine and 44 DIN hp. VW rated the car with a top speed of 125 km/h. Disc brakes were installed in the front.

With a practiced eye, you could recognize the VW 1500 without seeing the badge on the car: modifications to the rear axle widened the rear track by 10 mm to 1350 mm. This car also had larger tail lights. Production began in 1967 after the factory vacation.

The 1970 models didn't look too much different from the 1969 cars, at least for the European versions; VW increased the number of ventilation slits in the rear engine cover. The sedan got the 10-slit engine cover that until then had only been used in the Cabriolet. The open-air Beetle now had an engine cover with four groups of seven inlets. The reason for this change was the introduction in the US of the 1600 engine from the Type 3; this engine required more fresh air. With the appearance of the 1302, the VW 1500 with its old ball joint suspension disappeared from the model line.

The most important model changes and improvements VW 1500:

1966:	August, introduction of the VW 1500 with 44 DIN hp under the slogan, "VW 1300 now with 1500 engine and front disc brakes." Top speed 125 km/h; 0-100 km/h: 23s. Rear track: 1350 mm. Final drive: 4.125 (VW 1300: 4.375). Further changes same as for the VW 1300.
1967:	September, introduction of VW 1500 with automatic and new rear axle (semi-trailing links with double-joint drive shafts). Padded dashboard available at extra cost (DM 200). Front headrests, reverse lights, hazard lights, indicator lights, and rear window defroster.
1968:	Same as for VW 1300.
1969:	August, air inlets in engine cover, L package available. Otherwise same as for VW 1300.
1970:	July, model line discontinued, replaced by VW 1302.

VW 1302 (1970-72)

The VW 1302 came onto the scene in the autumn of 1970 with a longer front, a completely new front axle, and the semi-trailing link rear suspension from the automatic Beetle. None of VW's competition had installed such an expensive axle. From behind, the Beetle basically looked the same. Few people noticed the larger curve in the engine cover. From the front, it was obvious that changes had been made. The front trunk was enlarged from 140 liters (4.9 ft^3) to 260 liters (9.2 ft^3) due to the new front axle with MacPherson struts and the 63 mm wider front track. The spare tire was now completely under the trunk floor. The front hood was enlarged as well and had a larger curve. New fenders also added to the more powerful presence. The wheelbase increased by 20 mm. The new safety steering column with steering dampers was double-jointed with cardan (universal) joints. These improvements naturally added extra weight. The 1302 weighed 870 kg, 50 kg more than the old VW 1300. The well-known 1.3-liter engine was modified for use in the Super Beetle. Compression was increased, and output pumped up to 44 DIN hp.

Performance wasn't spectacular though. "In spite of modifications, the engine is still weak, noisy, uses too much fuel, adequate heat is not guaranteed, insurance rating makes it expensive." But, "The car can go 125 km/h" (*Mot* magazine). If this wasn't enough, a buyer could add DM 200 to the DM 5745 base price and get the 1302 with the S package. This added the 1.6-liter engine with its 50 DIN hp, which had taken over from the 1.5 flat-four and had been

Model: VW 1302L
Built: 1970-72
Engine: 4-cylinder, boxer
Valves: ohv, central camshaft
Displacement: 1285 cm^3
Bore x stroke: 77 x 69 mm
DIN horsepower (kW) @ rpm: 44 (32) @ 4100
Drive: rear wheels
Carburetion: one Solex 31 PICT-3
Transmission: 4F, 1R
Brakes: drums, f/r
Top speed: 122 km/h
Curb weight kg: 870
Tires: 5.60-15
Wheelbase: 2420 mm
Track f/r: 1379/1352 mm
L x W x H: 4080 x 1585 x 1500 mm

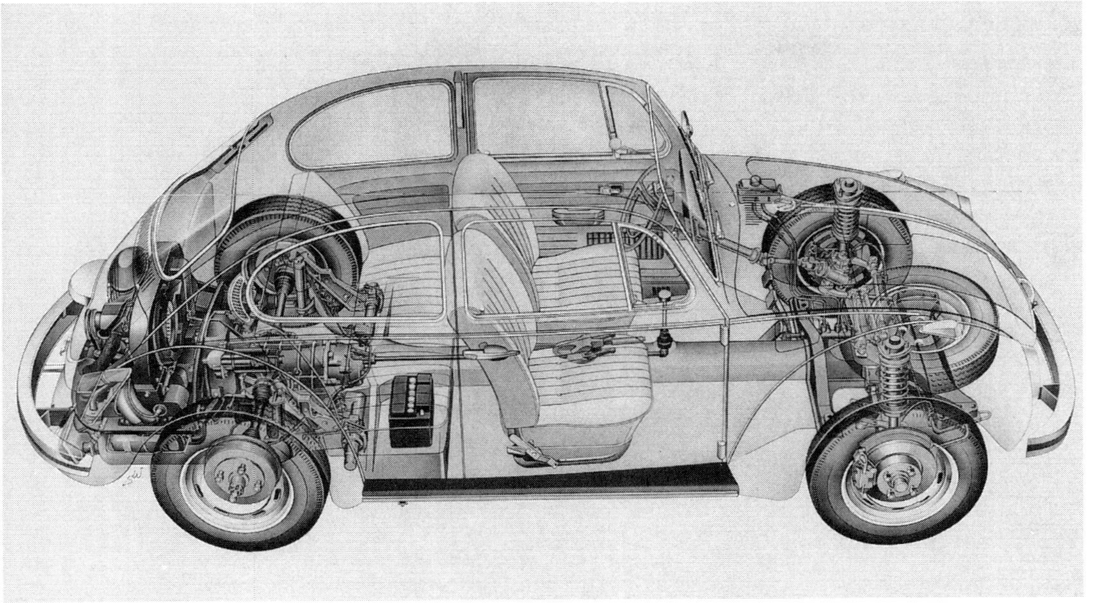

Cutaway view: VW 1302, model year 1970, with a strut suspension in the front and semi-trailing links in the rear. The wheelbase was increased for the first time; this is the reason VW used the "02."

sold in the US for the past two years. This new engine was a further modification of the 1.3-liter originally used in the VW 1600 Type 3, but modified to use the upright fan of the Beetle.

Both the 1300 and 1600 engine had a dual-port cylinder head. The lubrication system was also modified. The oil cooler was moved to the front. An additional thermostat installed in the air filter regulated the flow of warm air to the carburetor. Only the larger engine was used for export vehicles.

Changes made for the 1972 model year were not as drastic. The engine cover now had 26 air inlets (except for the base Beetle) and the water deflector plate was dropped. Volkswagen improved the protection of the electrical system from dampness, but a cold start in the rain or damp was still not one of the strengths of the

The total number of Type 1 registrations in 1971 (in Germany) broke down as follows: 67% of buyers bought either a 1302 or 1302S, 21% bought a VW 1300, 9% decided on a VW 1200, and 3% bought a Cabriolet. A total of 291,312 Beetles were sold that year in Germany.

Beetle. In contrast, there was much praise for the new chassis and for the double-jointed rear axle. It reduced the tendency of this classic car (which by the way on February 17, 1972 overtook the Ford Model T as the number one built car in the world) to oversteer. The natural tendency of a rear-heavy car only appeared when cornering at high speeds. The "best Beetle of all times" (according to the VW ads) only lasted two years until another facelift. These changes were so major that VW renamed the car.

VW 1303 (1972-75)

The 1303 with its wraparound windshield was at both the culmination and the end of Beetle development. Only the most outspoken Beetle experts will point out that a wraparound windshield wasn't appearing for the first time. Back in 1965, the windshield was slightly rounded. Thanks to its more radically curved windshield, the

Volkswagen-Porsche Austria prepared 1302S Beetles for use as rally cars. These cars pumped out 120 DIN hp and were entered as special touring cars in Group 2. They were quite successful.

The most important model changes and improvements VW 1302:

1970: August, introduction of 1302 (1.3-liter, 44 DIN hp, dual-port cylinder head) and 1302S (1.6-liter with 50 DIN hp). New front, 74 mm longer. Front axle with cross-tubes and torsion bars dropped in favor of suspension strut front axle with wishbones and stabilizer. Front trunk now 260 liter (9.2 ft³) with spare tire under floor. Modified trunk cover and fenders. Turning circle diameter, 9.60 m. Double-joint steering column, modified steering gear, three-section tie rods. Fuel tank holds 41.5 liters. Semi-trailing link rear axle instead of swing-arm axle, double-joint shafts. Front track increased by 69 mm, rear track by 2 mm. Wheelbase increased by 20 mm. Larger brake drum diameter. Disc brakes available as option. Forced ventilation.

1302S: Standard disc brakes. 1.6-liter double intake pipe and double-acting vacuum capsule. Dual-port cylinder head.

1971: August, fuel tank with baffle plate. Multi-function control stalk including wiper switch. Interval wipers available as extra cost option.

1972: August, model line discontinued, replaced by 1303.

Model: VW 1303L
Built: 1972-75
Engine: 4-cylinder, boxer
Valves: ohv, central camshaft
Displacement: 1285 cm³
Bore x stroke: 77 x 69 mm
DIN horsepower (kW) @ rpm: 44 (32) @ 4000
Drive: rear wheels
Carburetion: one Solex 31 PICT-3
Transmission: 4F, 1R
Brakes: drums, f/r
Top speed: 125 km/h
Curb weight: 890 kg
Tires: 5.60-15
Wheelbase: 2420 mm
Track f/r: 1379/1349 mm
L x W x H: 4140 x 1585 x 1500 mm

1303 looked much different from its predecessor, as seen from the front and from the side.

The new large, round taillights were a pronounced feature in the rear. These lights were quickly known, somewhat mockingly, as "elephant feet" and required new fenders. The three-chamber taillights were used to meet US safety regulations. They didn't make the rear of the Beetle any more beautiful, but it was easier to see. The windshield, and therefore the roof as well, were moved forward. This also provided an opportunity to modify the dashboard. Since 1958, all Beetle dashboards had been housed in steel frames. All changes made were cosmetic in nature, including new switches and padding. The new heavily padded vinyl dash with its larger binnacle for the speedometer. This gave passengers the impression of a larger interior. Shorter drivers, on the other hand, felt slightly walled in, as it was now harder to see over the dash.

The most powerful Beetle was the 1303LS. This model came with the 1.6-liter engine with 50 DIN hp and was (from the viewpoint of a Beetle) fully equipped. The front turn signals were installed in the fenders in 1975 models, but US, Canadian, and Japanese models remained the same due to costs. On the other hand, these Beetles were equipped with catalytic converters. Rack-and-pinion steering was also introduced this model year making a noticeable change for the better in the Beetle's handling. Although the old cam-and-roller steering had been continually modified (the last time in 1972), it still didn't give the driver enough feel for the

US safety regulations required a large number of changes, one of which led to the wraparound windshield. The regulation stated there had to a minimum distance between occupants and the windshield; this was designed to improve crash safety.

The Black and Yellow Racer: The air intake slits underneath the bumper were actually a feature of US models. This is where the heat exchanger core for the air conditioning was installed.

last time in 1972), it still didn't give the driver enough feel for the road, as it was always a little rubbery.

The 1303 was definitely not an inexpensive car. The base LS cost DM 6890. Many options which were recommended, and standard in many competitors' cars, cost extra in a VW. The following look at the options price list makes it clear that driving a Beetle was not necessarily an inexpensive hobby: radial tires, DM 132 to 144; rear window defroster, DM 55; steel sunroof, DM 295; rear center armrest, DM 37; parking heater, DM 353. One of the extras costs that Beetle buyers had to pay for was something that they gladly would have done without: the Beetle used quite a lot of fuel. If you drove fast in a 50 DIN hp Beetle, you could count on around 20 mpg. When driving for long distances at top speed on the highway, the Beetle got only 17 mpg on regular fuel, numbers that, even for a cult car, were too low.

Even given the fact that the 1303 was the best Beetle ever built, it had become outdated. "All of VW's efforts can't keep the successful Beetle from graying with age," (*Auto, Motor und Sport*).

In spite of the introduction of the Super Beetle, Beetle sales were dropping drastically. In 1973, 232,055 units were sold in Germany. In 1974, this number dropped by 50% to 118,915. In 1975, only 41,070 Beetles were sold. The decline continued, especially as the Golf, everything a modern car should be, had already been at VW dealers for quite some time. Only 15,914 Beetles were sold in Germany in 1976; the next year this number dropped to

In spite of enthusiastic ads and innumerable publicity promotions, the demise of the Beetle was unstoppable. These good-luck Beetles were given away as prizes on a German TV lottery show in 1974.

6524. Any expensive model changes were impossible with these sales figures. Wolfsburg reacted by removing the expensive 1303 models from the 1976 model line. If you wanted a Beetle, you had to buy the 1200 with the shorter front end. The wraparound windshield lived on in the Cabriolet. The Karmann Beetle had the longer front end until production ended.

VW Beetle Cabriolet Karmann (1949-80)

The Cabriolet was a VW tradition: A convertible was one of the three prototypes to be seen when the cornerstone of the then KdF factory was laid. Adolf Hitler liked to be seen in an open-air vehicle, which is about the only similarity to the man who would be running the factory eight years later. Major Ivan Hirst was also a convertible buff, whose official car was a Cabriolet.

Volkswagen had been building the Export Beetles in Emden since 1964. These 1303 models were headed for the US. The turn signals give away their destination.

The most important model changes and improvements VW 1303:

1972: August, introduction of VW 1303. Wraparound windshield moved forward. New dashboard with rocker switches (previously pull knobs). Fresh-air outlets across entire width of vehicle. Fuse box in center of dashboard, new seats. Finger aperture for filler flap cover dropped. Defroster outlets on left and right. Triple-chamber taillights. Engine basically unchanged.

US model included exhaust gas recirculation (EGR) system. DM 6890.

October, modified carburetor.

1973: January, special edition "Yellow and black racer": 1303S with black hood and trunk, sport steering wheel and seats, steel 5.5J x 15 wheels, 175/70 HR 15 tires. 3500 built. DM 7650.

August, introduction of 1303A with 34 DIN hp/1.2-liter engine, simplified interior. Front axle with negative offset for improved braking. More powerful AC alternator.

September, special edition "City Beetle" (1303/1.3-liter), Ibiza Red, Ischia Metallic, Ontario Metallic. Pinstripes, special seat fabric, carpeting. Automatic seatbelts, radio, special steering wheel, lockable engine cover, rubber trim on bumper, reverse lights. DM 7440.

Special edition "Big Beetle" (1303/1.6-liter), Hellas, Ontario or Moon Metallic, pinstripes. Otherwise same as City Beetle. Also, wood-grain film on dashboard; sport shift lever. 5.5 J x 15 wheels and steel-belted radials. DM 7670.

1974: August, 1303A dropped but 34 DIN hp still available. Front turn signals integrated in bumper. Tow lugs on bumper. Ribbed license plate light housing. Convex rear apron, black tailpipes (previously chrome-plated).

Rack-and-pinion steering introduced.

For US and Japan, 1.6 liter/50 DIN hp with fuel injection and catalytic converter.

1975: July, production of VW 1303 ends.

Rudolf Ringel designed the open-air Beetle. He worked at Porsche and later in Wolfsburg as head of testing. He basically copied the pre-WWII KdF Cabriolet and built two or three prototypes classified as Type 15 cars. The windshield and window frames were from the sedan which is why the windows often broke when the high-quality and snug-fitting top was opened and closed. The semaphore indicators were installed, as on the military's Kübelwagen, on the A pillar. They were installed on the B pillar when the car went into production.

When Karmann first approached Volkswagen to ask them for a chassis to use to build a Cabriolet is unknown. What is known is when the British finally gave in. The 10,000th post-war Beetle was supposedly delivered to the Karmann factory in Osnabrück in

November 1946. The occupying forces sent cars there for maintenance and repairs.

Karmann's roots go back to 1874 when they built carriages during the boom following the founding of Germany. They built their first automobile body in 1902. At the beginning of WWII, Karmann had 600 workers on the payroll and was one of the largest makers of automobile bodies in Germany.

After 1946, Karmann built two Cabriolet prototypes, one with landau bars and one without. Neither car had a rear window. Numerous reinforcements made these Cabriolets torsionally stiff but also heavier, by 40 kg, with the obvious negative effect on the Cabriolet's performance.

Heinrich Nordhoff devoted himself to the Cabriolet in 1949; Karmann built a third prototype followed by a pre-production run of 25. The cars were put through a very difficult 20,000-km test that ended on August 5, 1949. The final report rated these cars very high; they definitely met Volkswagen's standards. Following this, Nordhoff placed an order for 2000 (some say 1000) with Karmann. The cars were built, of course, with a large percentage of VW parts. The new Cabriolet was known as the Type 15 and was based on the Export Beetle, never on the Standard model.

The first production VW Cabriolet appeared in June 1949. By the end of that year, an additional 363 were built. The semaphore indicators moved to a position behind the doors starting with chassis number 361. This change was due to the weak area near

The convertible version of the KdF car. This car, with chassis number 31, has withstood all tests of time. It can be seen today, with over half a million kilometers on the odometer, in the Volkswagen museum in Wolfsburg. The first owner of the car was Adolf Hitler.

Various convertible prototypes were built while VW was still administered by the British. The cars differ mainly in the way the top is constructed. The photo shows one of the three Karmann protoypes. This one had landau bars.

After Karmann had built 25 pre-production convertibles in 1948, Heinrich Nordhoff placed an order for 2000 in 1949. The car went into production June 3, 1949. These early Cabriolets had semaphore indicators on the A pillar just as the earlier open-air KdF cars had.

Model year 1951: Semaphore indicators on the B pillar, no sun visors, and the hubcaps with the VW emblem in body color (used between 1949 and 1956).

The first sales brochure for the Karmann convertible did not mention Volkswagen: "German drivers have had a special long-standing preference for this body shape."

the windshield where additional reinforcements had to be added. A sturdy cross-member was welded into the area under the rear seat. Massive box-section supports were installed to reinforce the rocker panels. Karmann reinforced the front side panels from the inside using additional double-walled panels. The rear side windows could be lowered, whereas the first Beetle Cabriolets, as well as the KdF cars of course, had simple side screens.

The front hood and fenders came from the sedan while the engine cover was slightly modified. The air inlets, normally located just underneath the rear window, moved further down onto the engine cover itself. There were a total of 36 slits, 18 on each side. At that time, the inlets were vertical. Over the years, the number and position of air inlets changed. This was one of the

Model: Type 151 Cabriolet
Built: 1949-53
Engine: 4-cylinder, boxer
Valves: ohv, central camshaft
Displacement: 1131 cm^3
Bore x stroke: 75 x 64 mm
DIN horsepower (kW) @ rpm: 25 (18) @ 3300
Drive: rear wheels
Carburetion: one Solex 26 VFJ
Transmission: 4F, 1R
Brakes: drums, f/r
Top speed: 105 km/h
Curb weight kg: 800
Tires: 5.00-16
Wheelbase: 2400 mm
Track f/r: 1290/1250 mm
L x W x H: 4050 x 1540 x 1500 mm

1952 dashboard: A new dashboard was introduced along with sun visors made of tinted plastic.

1954 model: The special characteristic of the Karmann convertibles was the perfect fit of the top. It supposedly took four hours to install, and required two people to do it. At first, only one to two cars were built per day.

This is a 1957 convertible built for the US. This can be recognized by the large bumper with overriders (first available in 1955), the special turn signals, and the whitewall tires.

1961 model: An interior view of a VW 1200 Cabriolet. Karmann opened a new factory in Osnabrück that year as they were now building bodies for Porsche along with the Cabriolet and Ghia cars for VW.

Model: VW 1300 Cabriolet
Built: 1965-66
Engine: 4-cylinder, boxer
Valves: ohv, central camshaft
Displacement: 1285 cm^3
Bore x stroke: 77 x 69 mm
DIN horsepower (kW) @ rpm: 40 (29) @ 4000
Drive: rear wheels
Carburetion: one Solex 30 PICT-1
Transmission: 4F, 1R
Brakes: drums, f/r
Top speed: 122 km/h
Curb weight kg: 820
Tires: 5.60-15
Wheelbase: 2400 mm
Track f/r: 1305/1300 mm
L x W x H: 4070 x 1540 x 1500 mm

very few changes that was sometimes different for the sedan and the Cabriolet. Any improvements made to the Export sedan usually found their way into the Cabriolet. In 1957, for instance, the air inlets (2 x 5) were horizontal, while 12 years later there were a total of 28 horizontal inlets (4 x 7). In 1972, there were only 26. The convertible top was also different for this model, as well as for the 1303 Cabriolet in 1973. The window mechanism was a Cabriolet specialty.

The top, developed and built by Karmann, always received a lot of praise. It made the VW Cabriolet, unlike others, a convertible that could be driven the entire year. This is something that makes the VW Convertible special even today. The multi-layer top surrounded a complicated wood and steel frame, and it was this combination that made a convertible with the top up as quiet as a sedan. The convertible top itself consisted of three layers, the roof liner, the horsehair padding and the linen outer skin. The rear window, at first as small as a mail slot, was enlarged in October 1952 and then in 1958 by 47%. No further enlargements were made until 1976, when VW increased the window area by 12%.

From the start, the Cabriolet came in a number of attractive color combinations, with the top usually a different color than the convertible body. The front seats came from the sedan, while the rear seat was somewhat narrower in the Cabriolet due to the side reinforcements. The carpeting was also cut differently. Leather seats were available at extra cost only for the Cabriolet.

A new look, with proven technology: The 1967 VW 1500 Cabriolet came with all the model changes the sedan had undergone. The flat hubcaps were introduced in 1965.

From the Export Cabriolet to the 1303LS

Until 1991, the VW had the largest production run of any convertible: 331,847 were built between June 1949 and January 1980. The Cabriolet sold for a long time but was not necessarily a bestseller. On average, 10,000 were sold each year, a fairly low number for a mass-production car. For a classic car, on the other hand, this was a lot.

As stated above, the first Beetle Cabriolet appeared in June 1949. By April 1950, half of the Cabriolets VW ordered had sold. In February 1951, Wolfsburg placed an order for 2000 more; by the end of that year Karmann had built 4009 open-air Beetles. Most of the Cabriolets were sold to the Swiss, with only a few remaining in Germany. This is no surprise considering the Karmann Cabriolet, at DM 7500, was about 50% more expensive than the Beetle. The magazine *Auto und Kraftrad* compared the costs of the various Beetle models in their July 1954 issue. The Cabriolet cost DM 6500 (this included DM 6126 for a Cabriolet without tires and DM 374 for the tires). The vehicle tax was DM 216. Add to that DM 160 for liability insurance and DM 26 for fire and theft insurance. The insurance tax was DM 9.30. Altogether the testers under chief engineer Paul figured yearly fixed costs of DM 1681 for the Cabriolet and DM 1287 for the Standard Beetle. Perhaps this is why the Volkswagen Cabriolet remained in the shadow of the (less-expensive) Beetle with the steel roof.

The 1971 VW 1302LS listed for DM 7990. Optional special colors were now available at extra cost, exclusively for the Cabriolet. A Cabriolet customer could order from the Porsche color palette as well as from the VW colors. Cabriolet buyers could, however, choose between leatherette and cloth seats at no extra cost.

The automobile press finally took real notice of the convertible Beetle at the end of the 1960s. *Auto, Motor und Sport* tested the 44 DIN hp Karmann Cabriolet with the 1500 engine and auto-stick transmission in their 10/1968 issue. That car cost DM 6894 with the top down and had a relatively low top speed of 110 km/h. "The money spent on this Cabriolet is well worth it, if you enjoy driving with the top down and need room for four people," according to the two-page article. They also tested the 1302 and 1303 Cabriolets, the best-loved models in the convertible series. In the previous ten years, 125,411 of the Cabriolets with the larger front end had been built.

This is understandable if you believe what test reports at the time were saying. "The folding top does not take away, in any respect, the typical roundness of the Beetle. On the contrary, it gives the car a particular charm. . . . With the top down, though, the Cabriolet's occupants are hit with the more or less strong wind blowing through the interior. . . . With the top up, the Cabriolet also makes a good impression. The roof is absolutely leak tight and easy to use, while the interior roof trim makes for a cozy interior. The performance of the 50 DIN hp 1.6-liter is not exactly spectacular but is definitely adequate." Only adequate? "The 50 DIN hp engine in the rear provides satisfactory performance. The Cabriolet can run up to 130 km/h with 0 to 100 km/h in 21.5 seconds." This quote is from a 1303 test report in *Auto, Motor und Sport* published three months earlier.

Top restoration: a 1303 Cabriolet, first registered in April 1976. The base price then, not counting the 11% tax, was DM 10,927.93. With the options installed, the price of this rose to DM 13,306. The 5-inch ATS wheels and the Cibie driving lights installed later are typical accessories of the that time.

The testers from the magazine *Mot* also devoted themselves to testing the Cabriolet. In the spring of 1971, Dr. Paul Simsa tested a 1302LS Cabriolet, the "last sanctuary for romantics" and came to the following conclusion. "The driver of an open-air Beetle gets more out of the car." Two years later, Simsa renewed his acquaintance with the 1303LS Cabriolet that had just been added to the *Mot* test fleet. This time he said, "The VW Cabriolet is a relatively expensive love interest with several negatives speaking against it. "And these are, Dr. Simsa?" High price, much higher than the cost of a sedan (with higher depreciation). Ventilation with the top up is worse than the sedan with a sunroof. Interior gets very dirty. General disadvantages of a Cabriolet (safety, life span). Replacing

Fully loaded from the options and accessories list: Lockable filler flap (DM 17.20), rear defroster (DM 136.94), radial ply tires (DM 202.70), spare tire (steel-belted, DM 45.95), automatic seatbelts (DM 55.86), adjustable headrests (DM 92.79), passenger-side mirror (DM 21.61), halogen headlights (DM 105.41) and interval wipers (DM 34.23).

The LS designation was dropped from the 1303 in 1975 as the 50 DIN hp was now the only engine available for the Cabriolet. The 5.5 x 15 sport wheels with 175/70 SR 15 tires were available starting in 1978 at extra cost. The standard wheel/tire combination for the Cabriolet: 165 tires on 4.5-inch rims.

Model:
VW 1303LS Cabriolet
Built: 1972-80
Engine: 4-cylinder, boxer
Valves: ohv, central camshaft
Displacement: 1584 cm^3
Bore x stroke: 85.5 x 69 mm
DIN horsepower (kW) @ rpm:
50 (37) @ 4000
Drive: rear wheels
Carburetion:
one Solex 34 PICT-3
Transmission: 4F, 1R
Brakes:
front discs, rear drums
Top speed: 130 km/h
Curb weight kg: 940
Tires: 5.60-15
Wheelbase: 2420 mm
Track f/r: 1394/1349 mm
L x W x H:
4140 x 1585 x 1500 mm

the top is expensive. One sits too low in the car, view to the rear is poor both with the top up and down." But that really can't be too bad. "The only people who are interested in the VW Cabriolet are individualists who want a convertible with four seats."

But if you wanted a four-seater convertible, you really didn't have much of a choice available on the German market. Really the only other option was to visit your bank and then make a trip to your friendly Rolls-Royce dealer, where you could plunk down DM 190,000 for a four-seater convertible with a roll bar. This was the stylish Corniche. For that kind of money, you could buy a dozen Beetle Cabriolets (base price in 1978: DM 13,374).

When the last Beetle Cabriolet came off the assembly line on January 10, 1980, demand for the Cabriolet quickly increased, particularly when it became known that the successor would have a

Karmann built their last open-air Beetle in January 1980. In the final years, the Cabriolet with its wraparound windshield was only built for the American market. The Cabriolet was saying a slow good-bye there, and VW was offering a number of special models— the Sun Bug, Champagne Edition, Triple Black and Triple White (shown in photograph).

roll bar. "Henkelmann?—nein Danke" (Convertible with roll bar?—no thanks!) stated the yellow and black stickers of Beetle activists. Resistance to the Cabriolet with a roll bar has long been silent, but many fans still dream of an open 1303, in particular, one with Cibie driving lights and five-spoke ATS rims.

The most important model changes and improvements VW Cabriolet:

Changes same as the Type 1 Export, plus the following:

1949: June, Karmann Cabriolet Type 15 introduced: Four-seater Cabriolet based on Export model, built by Karmann. Mechanics same as Type 1 sedan, DM 7500.

1952: October, larger rear window.

1953: January, new dashboard, glove compartment with lockable cover on right.

August, bare window trim, insignia "Karmann-Kabriolett." Golden Wolfsburg coat of arms in center of steering wheel.

1956: August, adjustable rearview mirror, leatherette and trim for interior door and side trim.

1957: August, horizontal cooling air inlets, modified convertible top frame. Chrome trim on dashboard. Larger rear window.

1959: August, modified top, rear part of top removable including window.

1960: April, tension cable in top, aluminum-colored trim on peak of hood dropped. 11,921 Cabriolets built (new record for a year's production).

1962: New Karmann insignia.

1964: August, modified top, modified retaining hooks, interior light on top of windshield frame. PVC top. Doors slightly lower.

1966: New rubber seals for rear side windows.

1967: August, modified top, new top securing mechanism. Safety glass rear window.

1969: August, 28 air inlets in engine cover. 10-digit chassis number.

1971: August, introduction of 1302LS Cabriolet. 26 air inlets. 24,317 Cabriolets built.

1972: Modified top.

1973: August, introduction of 1303LS.

1975: New seat material and padding.

1980: January, last Beetle Cabriolet (chassis number 152 044 140) comes off assembly line. A total of 331,847 Karmann Beetle Cabriolets were built.

VW Hebmüller-Cabriolet (1949-53)

The Hebmüller-Cabriolet had a famous predecessor, the Radclyffe Roadster, built when the factory was still run by British occupation forces. This was a two-seater that looked almost the same from the front as from the rear.

This well-designed two-seater had its roots in a suggestion made by Colonel Michael McEvoy, who worked for a small British Mercedes racing team before the war. He actually wanted to see a Volkswagen racecar be built, but this was rejected by Major Hirst. The idea, though, got into the minds of other people, such as Rudolf Ringel, who had developed the four-seater Beetle Cabriolet for Ivan Hirst. He put a lot of thought into a possible two-seater built on the sedan's platform. Hirst's sports car had two almost identical hoods: one in the front covering the trunk and another, albeit slightly modified, in the rear. The rear hood formed part of the rear of the car as well as serving as the engine cover. The Roadster looked a lot like the later Hebmüller Cabriolet. Hirst himself never entertained a thought about who was the father of the Hebmüller convertible. The Hebmüller people who toured the Volkswagen factory to work out a deal with VW probably let themselves be inspired by the Radclyffe Roadster. This car with its two carburetors was the preferred means of transport of Colonel Charles Radclyffe, Hirst's boss.

Hebmüller was founded in 1889 by Joseph Hebmüller in Wuppertal as a carriage builder. His four sons took over the company after Joseph died in 1919 and gradually turned it into an automobile manufacturer. They began by modifying already-existing bodies, and then took the relatively small step to building their own designs. As an automobile manufacturer, Hebmüller's sons became known for their two- and four-seater convertibles. Even the British occupying forces had convertibles built at the Hebmüller factory. In 1948, the Wuppertal-based factory got hold of something they had

This is a photo of the Radclyffe Roadster, only one of which was ever built. Ivan Hirst commissioned it for Charles Radclyffe. The car was used as a model for the two-seater Hebmüller. Two Roadster bodies were allegedly built, as the body from Roadster No. 1 was said to have been irreparably damaged in an accident.

Picture perfect: Title page from the Hebmüller brochure. This car was actually sold as a Volkswagen Cabriolet, unlike the Karmann four-seater, whose connection to VW was not mentioned.

wanted for a while: a Volkswagen body. Karmann and Hebmüller were contracted to design and build Cabriolet prototypes: Karmann built a four-seater and Hebmüller a two-seater. To save costs, they were to use as many parts from the sedan as possible. Three prototypes were built at first.

The two hoods that looked alike became a typical characteristic of the Hebmüller Roadster, but they were actually quite different. The engine cover on the first prototype seems to be not quite

The back of the Hebmüller brochure; after the fire, production never really got back up and running. Karmann built 12 Roadsters from parts left over after production ended. Two more were built later.

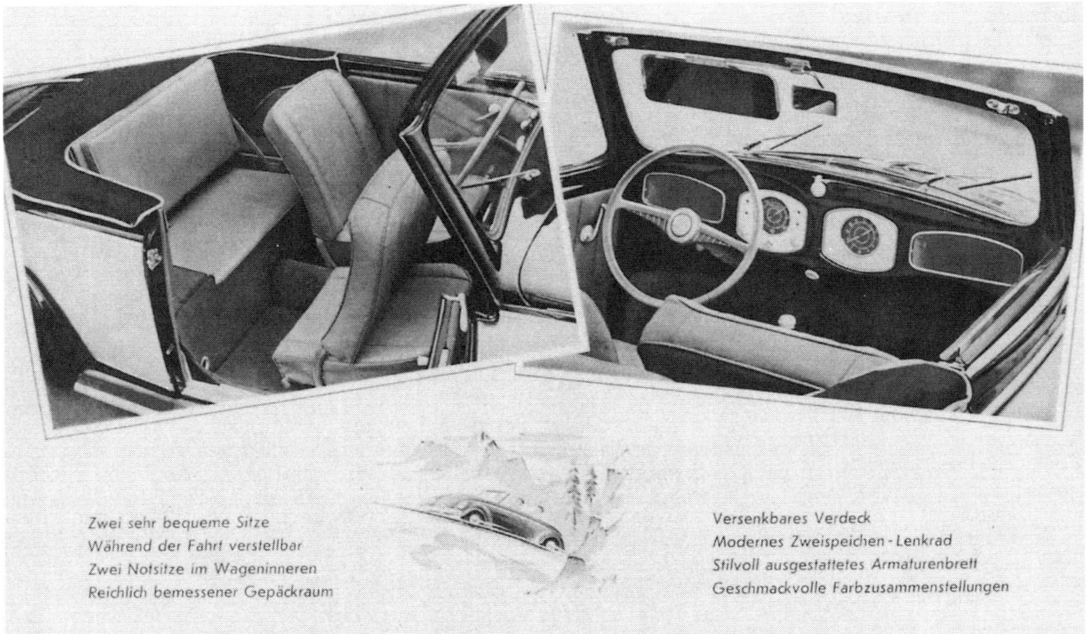

Model: Type 14A Hebmüller
Built: 1949-53
Engine: 4-cylinder, boxer
Valves: ohv, central camshaft
Displacement: 1131 cm^3
Bore x stroke: 75 x 64 mm
DIN horsepower (kW) @ rpm: 25 (18) @ 3300
Drive: rear wheels
Carburetion: one Solex 26 VFJ
Transmission: 4F, 1R
Brakes: drums, f/r
Top speed: 100 km/h
Curb weight kg: 775
Tires: 5.00-16
Wheelbase: 2400 mm
Track f/r: 1290/1250 mm
L x W x H: 4050 x 1540 x 1500 mm

Even a Hebmüller coupe was planned; a prototype was even built. The catastrophic fire put an end to any further plans.

finished, with its four cooling slits on either side. The other two prototypes had five air inlets on each side. The engine cover for all three Roadsters was quite heavy and had a pronounced centerline with chrome trim. The license plate lights and the single brake light used on all three prototypes came from the sedan.

Although basically the same, each prototype was unique. For example, the first Roadster had the banana-shaped bumper over-riders from the original sedan, while the other two were equipped with the stronger bumpers used between 1946 and 1953. For sufficient body stiffness, Hebmüller reinforced the body and floor with side members underneath the rocker panels, installed a z-shaped panel behind the front seats, and reinforced the rear side panels and floor. They used a tubular frame to prevent window fracture.

The Roadster prototypes were then put to the test. Even after 10,000 km of testing they were still in great shape. Volkswagen was impressed and ordered 2000 units, known as Type 14A cars.

Although the production cars were basically identical (technically and mechanically) to the prototypes and the sedans, there were some important differences. Perhaps the most important was that the production Roadster didn't have the large steel nose in the rear. Instead it had a well-designed sculpted line that extended down the entire front hood. The license plate lights were still installed at the end of this line. In addition, the air inlets moved off the engine cover and just in front of the engine, into the area between the cover and the roof.

The Roadster was known as one of the most beautiful post-war cars. The first VW two-seaters were delivered on July 1, 1949, and were available from the factory in two-tone paint, as the Karmann Cabriolets were. By the end of that year, an almost identical number of Hebmüller Cabriolets (358) and Karmann Cabriolets (360) had been built. Production was running at full speed at 2:00 pm on the afternoon of Saturday, July 23, 1949, when a fire broke out in the paint shop. The wind drove the fire throughout the factory. Part of the roof caved in, destroying the production facilities and the machine tools; only a few items were saved. The cause of the fire was never discovered.

Production began again four weeks later, but Hebmüller hadn't enough insurance. In spite of the number of orders, they were never really able to get back on their feet. By January 1950 they had only built an additional 125 cars. One hundred were built in February, another 77 in March and a miserable seventeen in April. Production then came to a halt and only restarted in August 1951. One Roadster was built. In May 1952, Hebmüller declared bankruptcy. Karmann got any leftover parts and built twelve more (some other sources say fourteen) Cabriolets at their factory in Osnabrück. The end came in February 1953.

If Volkswagen numbers are correct, exactly 696 Type 14A models were sold; Hebmüller records show 750 were built.

Besides the Roadster, Hebmüller also built a special police car, the Type 18A. Although the car seems more than a bit strange today with its canvas doors and lumpy roof, German police used them up to the mid-1950s. Papler and Austro-Tatra also built police Cabriolets. Between 1948 and 1960, 2105 VW police cars were built.

Brand-new Hebmüller Roadsters again became available in the mid-80s when Leo Nijmann from the Netherlands built a replica based on the Mexican Beetle, which looked a lot like the original.

Top left:
Type 18A: This police convertible, built by Hebmüller, was also available from Volkswagen. Papler and Austro-Tatra built similar cars.

Hebmüller offered the Type 14A in many tasteful dual-tone colors. By the way, the trunk lid was not identical to the engine cover.

The large rear engine cover was made of modern plastic. Mass production of the car never got going. Since 1994, Veedub Australia in Victoria has been building Roadsters based on the Beetle sedans built in Australia between 1954 and 1976.

VW Karmann-Ghia Type 14 (1955-1974)

At the beginning of 1950, Karmann began negotiations with Volkswagen to build a sports car for them. The first meeting between Dr. Wilhelm Karmann, son of the company founder, Dr. Feuereisen, VW vice president and Ludwig Boehner, head of development at VW, didn't produce any results. Three years later,

June 1940

March 1946

March 4, 1950

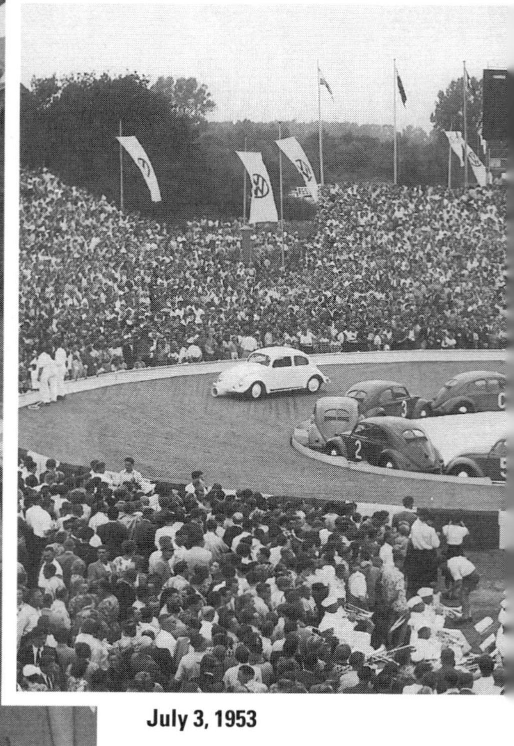

July 3, 1953

Chronicle of a World Champion

August 5, 1955

February 17, 1972

January 19, 1978

May 15, 1981

however, in the autumn of 1953, Volkswagen showed an interest when Wilhelm Karmann presented them with a sports car built by Ghia, a company based in Turin, Italy.

Giacinto Ghia's design studio had been run since 1948 by Felice Mario Boano, a friend of the car design artist who had died in 1944. Since 1951 they had tailored designs from Chrysler and its chief designer, Virgil Exner. Many of their show car designs had taken shape in Turin. Exner would later maintain that the Karmann silhouette closely resembled one of his designs, the K-310 study from 1953. The Ghia business director also wanted to do work for

Between 1951 and 1961 Ghia built many design studies and prototypes for Chrysler. The Karmann-Ghia presented in 1955 was similar to the Chrysler K-310 Pate study. The front end reminded one of a 1947 Alfa.

Volkswagen, but they never got a body from VW to work on. Nordhoff had prohibited the sale of individual bodies. The Italians did eventually get a platform from Charles Labouche, the French VW and Chrysler agent.

The first sketches of the car that would be introduced as the VW coupe in 1955 were drawn by Mario Boano probably at the beginning of the 1950s. The Karmann front reminded one of an Alfa Romeo design done in 1947. The Ghia prototype was shown to Wilhelm Karmann at the Paris auto show in October 1953. The negotiations he then began with Heinrich Nordhoff led to the following decision: Karmann would take care of production and final assembly while VW would handle the engineering and the distribution.

The costs of modifying the Beetle were reasonable. The new body only required that the floor pans be widened by 80 mm on each side, the steering column be slightly lower, and the shift lever be shortened. The final point was due to the lower seating position. The car slowly got closer to being ready for production during 1954. Karmann's biggest problem was that they didn't have the presses they needed. Building a Ghia body was a complicated business. The front of the coupe alone consisted of five different pieces that had to be welded together; a Ghia body was composed of dozens of pieces of formed sheet metal. Karmann made minor changes for production purposes, such as adding additional air inlets in the front, building a one-piece bumper instead of the planned two-piece, and moving the front signal lights to a position directly under the headlights.

The car was introduced to the press on July 14, 1955, just before the VW factory vacation began. The public introduction was at the Internationale Automobilausstellung (IAA-International Car Show) in Frankfurt in September. Five hundred cars were built that year. Ten thousand units were built the next year. Karmann amazingly was able to keep up with demand for the new car even though they were also building the Beetle Cabriolet in parallel on the same production lines.

At DM 7500, the Karmann-Ghia was expensive, but the stylish Beetle found its own niche in the sports car market, even if it really wasn't a very sporty car. As part of a look at the sports cars available on the German market in 1967, *Auto, Motor und Sport* wrote, "The shape of the VW Karmann-Ghia is the only reason it appears in this article. In terms of performance, these cars with their standard VW engines lie far behind the current level of sports cars available. . . .This car proves that German buyers are willing to pay for Italian shapes particularly when the car, like this one, is based on a solid platform."

"The seats are well-sprung and supportive," as the sales brochure described them. They also referred to the "non-slip rubber accelerator pedal cover . . . the right size for any size heel of a ladies' shoe." That actually came later as this picture is from 1955 and shows the typical Beetle gas pedal. The leatherette interior cost extra.

Karmann-Ghia Coupe

The Karmann-Ghia was supposed to give buyers the feeling they were driving an exotic car without requiring them to pay the high cost of maintenance that type of car usually requires. Cars built according to this principle were few and far between. This made the Karmann-Ghia somewhat of a sensation; the fact that Beetle engineering lay underneath the elegant body was left unmentioned. When the coupe premiered in 1955, it was equipped with the Beetle's well-known 1192 cm^3, 30 DIN hp engine. The only difference was the relocation of the air filter. Due to the low beltline, the oil-bath air filter was replaced by the air filter from the VW bus and installed on the left side of the engine compartment. This change required the use of a different carburetor. In addition, the 6-volt battery was installed in the engine compartment and not, as in the Beetle, underneath the rear seat. Any mechanical changes VW made to the Beetle made their way into the Ghia, traditionally in August at the start of every model year. The only differences between the cars, besides the shape, had to do with the interior appointments and standard options; they tended toward luxury in the Ghia.

The reasons to buy a Beetle were also the reasons to buy a Karmann-Ghia: excellent build quality, simplicity and reliability, large number of dealers, and an excellent supply of spare parts. Although the Karmann and the Beetle had the same mechanical underpinnings, the coupe seemed much more agile. Its center of gravity and seating position created the atmosphere of a sports car. Even professional test teams were of the same opinion. *Auto, Motor und Sport* suspected that "VW engines were carefully selected for use in the Karmann." *Road & Track*, required reading

Model: VW 1200 Karmann-Ghia Coupe
Built: 1955-59
Engine: 4-cylinder, boxer
Valves: ohv, central camshaft
Displacement: 1192 cm^3
Bore x stroke: 77 x 64 mm
DIN horsepower (kW) @ rpm: 30 (22) @ 3400
Drive: rear wheels
Carburetion: one Solex 28 PICT-1
Transmission: 4F, 1R
Brakes: drums, f/r
Top speed: 118 km/h
Curb weight kg: 820
Tires: 5.60-15
Wheelbase: 2400 mm
Track f/r: 1290/1250 mm
L x W x H: 4140 x 1634 x 1330 mm

for many US drivers, came to a similar conclusion, "We felt somehow, for whatever reason, that the coupe runs better than the sedan." Feelings aside, in reality, the Karmann-Ghia wasn't really much faster than the Beetle. For this reason, some people felt something needed to be done about this. A letter written by Peter Schallhorn, a reader from Kiel to the editors of the magazine *Automobil* was published in their 4/1959 issue. "Can the engine from the Porsche 356A (1660 cm^3, 60 DIN hp) be installed in the Karmann-Ghia?" The response was not promising, "It would be possible, but a Porsche engine requires Porsche brakes and the certification office would most likely reject this combination." Instead, the magazine recommended Okrasa tuning ("costs just over DM 1000"). This modification would supposedly raise the top speed to 145 km/h, which was more than enough. "Driving faster than 160 km/h in a Karmann is not recommended, it is almost a bit foolish as the chassis is only designed for 110 km/h." Underneath the Italian tailored suit was true solid German conservativeness. At least the car seemed quite comfortable.

The body (interior width 1400 mm compared to the Beetle at 1215 mm) was comfortable and roomy. Once you sat inside though you were reminded of the sedan thanks to the high beltline. This could also be due to numerous components Karmann took from the

The engine in the rear of the Karmann was the well-known 30 DIN hp 4-cylinder air-cooled boxer engine. Many buyers thought it was underpowered as the car's top speed was only 120 km/h, not much faster than the Beetle.

With the 40-liter fuel tank and the "tubeless balloon tire" (used as a spare tire) in the trunk there wasn't much room left for large pieces of luggage. The situation of course wasn't much different in the Beetle.

Wolfsburg parts bin: the two-spoke steering wheel with the "Wolfsburg Castle" in the center, the ashtray and speedometer were straight from the Beetle.

The Ghia cockpit, on the other hand, had a few more items that the Beetle sedan did without. For example, a large electric clock was installed next to the speedometer on the right of the steering column. The clock was "large enough to be able to be at home in someone's living room," according to *Auto, Motor und Sport.* All controls were easily accessible (turn signals at the left of the steering wheel), except the low-beam switch, which was located on the floor to the left of the clutch. The well-padded seats and the interior trim were covered in cloth. Leatherette for the seats, and a radio ,were available at extra cost. The rear seat was much narrower than the one installed in the Beetle (only 106 cm wide compared to 132 cm in the Beetle). Only two small children might feel comfortable there on a long trip. Rear headroom was also reduced quite a bit due to the coupe's roof. A better idea was to use this area as additional luggage space; the rear seatback could be folded down.

The Karmann-Ghia had the same trailing link front axle and rear swing axle found in the Beetle and VW bus. The coupe, on the other hand, came with a 12-mm stabilizer, something the Beetle didn't get

Model: VW 1300
Karmann-Ghia Coupe
Built: 1965-66
Engine: 4-cylinder, boxer
Valves: ohv, central camshaft
Displacement: 1285 cm³
Bore x stroke: 77 x 69 mm
DIN horsepower (kW) @ rpm:
40 (29) @ 4000
Drive: rear wheels
Carburetion:
one Solex 30 PICT-1
Transmission: 4F, 1R
Brakes: drums, f/r
Top speed: 128 km/h
Curb weight kg: 830
Tires: 5.60-15
Wheelbase: 2400 mm
Track f/r: 1305/1300 mm
L x W x H:
4140 x 1634 x 1330 mm

until five years later. This made a big difference in terms of handling, compared to the Beetle. The British magazine *Autosport* wrote, "The improvement in handling has to be experienced to be believed. The typical VW understeer is gone and one can actually drive fast on slick streets without having to worry about the tail wagging the dog. The up and down movement on bumpy roads is also gone. Weight distribution has obviously been improved and the center of gravity has been lowered." It is true that weight distribution had changed. Fifty-seven percent of the Beetle's weight was on the rear axle whereas this was increased to 58.3% in the coupe.

The rear swing axle was still a point of dissension. During fast cornering the VW rear still swung toward the outside of the curve and oversteered. This combination of camber and toe-in changes surprised novice Ghia pilots, but it must be said that the Karmann handled better. This was something that the German test drivers agreed with their British colleagues on, that this was due to the standard stabilizers, the tires, and the lower center of gravity. Steering was via VW's well-known king-pin steering with two-piece tie rod. The worm steering gear developed by Porsche was attached to the upper front axle tube and was, at least according to the testers, lighter. "This seems to be because Karmann carefully modified the steering."

From the beginning, the Karmann-Ghia was equipped with a hydraulic brake system with simplex drums comprising two brake shoes at all four corners. "Adequate," and "for sporty driving totally sufficient," said the magazine *Motor-Rundschau* in 1965.

Karmann-Ghia 1300, introduced in 1965. The 1500 engine and front disc brakes were added the next year making the car "even sportier, even more exclusive," as VW ads told you.

One of the real weak points was the poor 6-volt lighting, which made every night drive an exercise in night blindness. Many Karmann-Ghia owners upgraded to a 12-volt system.

Compared to the sedan, the coupe weighed in at 80 kg more, at 800 kg. With its 30 DIN hp it reached a top speed of around 120 km/h. The Ghias with 34 DIN hp were only slightly faster. The variances during production must have been extreme, as *Auto, Motor und Sport* tested the car in 1961 and came up with a top speed of 125 km/h as an "average value." The Karmann-Ghia was also available that year with the auto-stick. "The Saxomat may make sense in the VW in certain cases, but both the VW and Karmann-Ghia shift easily and exactly with the regular clutch allowing one to drive better and safer." Buyers could therefore save themselves the auto-stick cost of DM 310 . This money (and a few hundred more) was better spent on a Karmann Cabriolet.

The Karmann-Ghia Cabriolet Type 141 was introduced at the 1957 IAA. The open 2+2 seater cost DM 8250. This picture shows one of the available options: a snap-down tonneau cover.

Karmann-Ghia Cabriolet

The Karmann-Ghia Coupe was a definite success. "A kingdom for this car" was Heinz Kranz's conclusion after he tested the car in 1955 for the September issue of *Das Automobil.* This and other positive reactions gave Karmann the impetus to build a Cabriolet version of the Coupe. Production began on August 1, 1957, with the first public introduction a month later at the IAA in Frankfurt. The reactions from the press and the public were uniformly positive, even if the Cabriolet cost, at DM 8250, exactly DM 750 more than the Coupe.

Karmann had been eyeing building an open two-seater for a long time and had built a prototype as early as 1954. With no roof, the body wasn't very rigid, so Karmann reinforced both the body and the chassis. They added additional reinforcing panels to the sills, further reinforcements to the area around the A pillar and on either side of the rear seat. In addition, reinforcements were added to form the compartment for the top.

The folding top was very easy to put up and down. A turn of the knob above the rearview mirror on the windshield (the "central crank" as the ad called it) released the two hooks that secured the top to the windshield frame. The convertible top then disappeared, neatly folded, behind the seats. The Ghia Cabriolet was saved from the unsightly top cover (that partially blocked airflow to the engine) installed in the four-seater Karmann Cabriolet.

The Cabriolet cost about twice as much as the Standard Beetle. The least expensive Porsche at the time cost DM 12,600, and a Beetle Cabriolet DM 5990. Between September 1957 and July 1974, 80,881 Cabriolets were built. Any improvements made to the

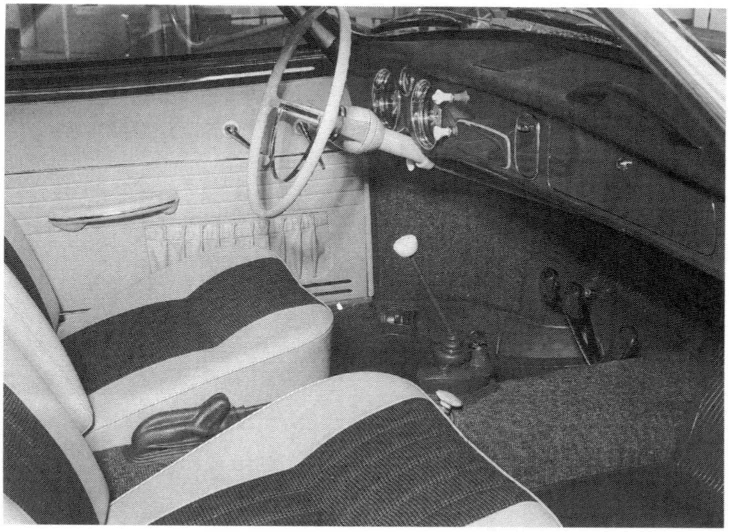

Karmann-Ghia interior, 1962. One of the available options can be seen in front of the shift lever: a transmission shift lock, supposed to deter potential thieves.

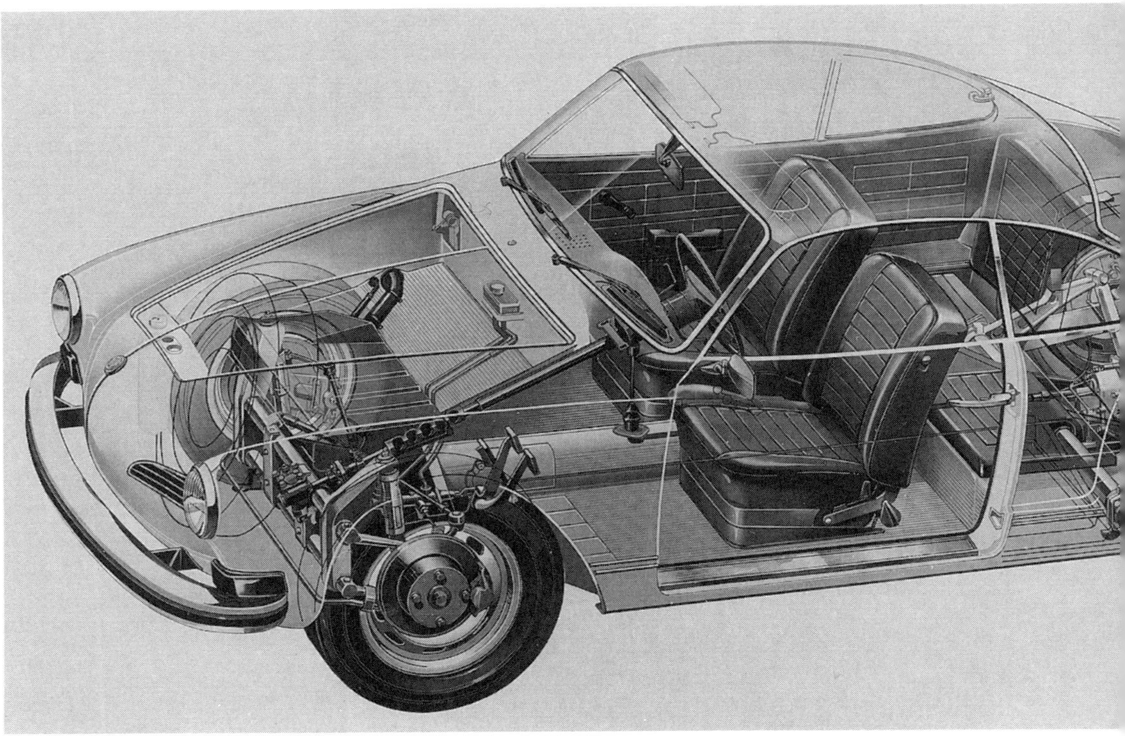

US safety regulations led to the last big facelift in 1971. Thanks to the modular design, VW was able to use some of the parts from the Type 3, such as the front turn signals and the taillights.

Elegant Beetle Twins: Both the sports coupe with the Italian Ghia body built by Karmann in Osnabrück and the Cabriolet still turn heads today.

For the 1960 model year the front and rear were modified. Distinguishing characteristics are the higher headlights and the wide, chrome air intake slits. This picture shows a 1963 Ghia Cabriolet with its 34 DIN hp engine installed in the rear. Many experts felt the design of this engine wasn't up to par as many camshaft breakages occurred.

Beetle were also made to the Karmann-Ghia. Both the Coupe and the Cabriolet got the 1285 cm^3, 40 DIN hp engine starting in 1966; a year later came the 1493 cm^3 with 44 DIN hp. The 50 DIN hp, 1584 cm^3 with 50 DIN hp from the 1302S was installed starting in 1970. Production for the German market ended in 1973. The last cars built for export rolled off the assembly line on June 21, 1974. The Osnabrück factory was then retooled for Scirocco production. A total of 443,466 Ghias were built; around a quarter of those were registered in Germany.

Karmann-Ghia production ended in July 1974. A total of 442,000 cars had been built since 1955, including 82,000 Cabriolets.

Model:
VW 1600 Karmann-Ghia
Built: 1970-74
Engine: 4-cylinder, boxer
Valves: ohv, central camshaft
Displacement: 1584 cm^3
Bore x stroke: 85.5 x 69 mm
DIN horsepower (kW) @ rpm:
50 (37) @ 4000
Drive: rear wheels
Carburetion:
one Solex 34 PICT-3
Transmission: 4F, 1R
Brakes: front discs,
rear drums
Top speed: 140 km/h
Curb weight kg: 870
Tires: 5.60 S 15
Wheelbase: 2400 mm
Track f/r: 1316/1350 mm
L x W x H:
4140 x 1634 x 1330 mm

Nice rear end: 1953 split window with Golde folding sunroof. The centerpiece between the windows was not a styling gag but a necessity. It was cheaper to produce the two smaller windows than one big rear window.

St 150-186
BS-EL 28

Collector's Edition Quote from an ad brochure of the time: "The car is at home in the flat countryside as in the mountains, on the highway as on back roads — whether business travel or bold travel plans. You are always safe and sound in the VW."

Top: Collector's item — VW 1300 Cabriolet from 1965.

One of a kind: Body by Hebmüller. Mass production of this car just wasn't possible after the devastating fire.

Top right: Museum piece — Type 51 in the Sinsheim Museum.

Middle right: Gem — beautifully restored 1955 Volkswagen Cabriolet.

Bottom right:
Criminal collector — police car in the car museum of the Stiftung Volkswagen (Volkswagen foundation).

Masterpiece: For many years, the Volkswagen Beetle was Germany's number one export. And this was almost the undoing of the Volkswagen factory in the first half of the 1970's. Between 1970 and 1975, sales in the American market plummeted by 50%. The low dollar exchange rate put the balance sheets deep in the red.

Above:
The first Transporter generation went into production in 1950 with an air-cooled rear engine, a trailing link suspension in the front and a swing axle in the rear. Around 1.8 million of them were built.

Upper right:
Whether van for the baker, plumber, or electrician, pickup for construction, bus, or ambulance; nothing happened in the economic miracle of Germany without one of these models.

Middle right:
The three rear-engine variations of the Volkswagen Transporter. On the right in the rear is the special edition T2 built from 1967 to 1979, sold in the USA as the "Champagne Edition."

**Below right:
The Kurierwagen (Type 181) wasn't only sold to the German army or the head forester, but also to institutions and official agencies.**

Breakdown:
These were even (occasionally) possible in a VW. If you didn't have the right tools on board, no problem. The nearest VW shop was never very far away. No other service network in Europe covered as much territory as VW's. In the 1960's there were over 6000 VW shops worldwide.

Right:
The car with the ironed crease: Karmann-Ghia 34 from the collection of the Stiftung AutoMuseum Wolfsburg. This museum is well worth visiting even if you aren't VW-crazed.

Below left:
One of a kind: The brochures were printed and the prices were set; however, the Type 3-based Karmann four-seater presented in 1961 never went into production.

Below right:
Ladies' choice: Woman in particular loved the Karmann-Ghia Cabriolet. The "sporty" Volkswagen cost in the last version it was sold, the 1600L, 8790 Marks. A total of 80,881 Cabriolets were built.

1969

Daring exploit: Volkswagen has always been good for a surprise. What is today the 12-cylinder sports car, was the VW-Porsche 914 in earlier years - just sensational. The first mass-produced mid-engine car was a joint development of Volkswagen and Porsche. The body of the 6-cylinder Porsche shown here was built by Karmann.

Sad news: When the long-awaited mid-size Volkswagen, the Type 4, appeared it wasn't the breakthrough that was expected. The concept of an air-cooled boxer engine in the rear had overstayed its welcome.

The most important model changes and improvements Karmann Ghia Type 14:

1955-74	Model changes same as the Type 1/VW Beetle. Introduced in August after the factory vacation, plus the following:
1953:	October, presentation of Coupe prototype in Paris.
1955:	July, production of Karmann-Ghia Coupe begins, press introduction. September, presented to public at IAA in Frankfurt.
1957:	IAA premiere of Cabriolet (Type 141). DM 8250. Fuel gauge standard. Turn signal switch with automatic return. Semi-circle horn ring on new steering wheel.
1959:	Headlights 45 mm higher and further forward. Door glass wider. Larger wheel arches, hinged rear side windows, passenger-side footrest, turn signal stalk with automatic return. Modified taillights, improved sound insulation, driver armrest, standard windshield washer and headlight flasher. Upper part of dashboard padded.
1960:	34 DIN hp engine introduced.
1961:	Transmission lock available as extra-cost option.
1964:	Interior light moved, now on bottom of rearview mirror.
1965:	Introduction of Karmann-Ghia with 1.3-liter engine (40 DIN hp). Windshield washer and light switch on left of speedometer. Main wiring harness in left side member (previously on right). Generator diameter 105 mm (previously: 90 mm). Modified brake drums.
1966:	August, all Karmann-Ghia models now with 1.5-liter engine and front disc brakes (dual-circuit brake system). Two-speed windshield wipers, modified door locks. New front seat shape, backrest adjustable to three different positions. Steering/ignition/starter lock instead of previous shift lock. Rear track increased, modified interior. Rear turn signal lens now orange (previously red).
1967:	Tank filler cap moved to front right. Auto-stick available. 12-volt electrical system.
1968:	Rear engine cover with water drain valve. 4.5J x 15 wheels. Hazard lights standard, warning lights with symbols.
1969:	Cabriolet now with glass rear window, previously plastic. Rectangular turn signals.
1970:	1.6-liter engine with 50 DIN hp. Rear window defroster, speedometer with trip odometer.
1971:	Rubber trim on bumper, taillights from Type 3. Instrumentation from Type 4, padded knee bar. Trim on lower part of front seats. Rear side windows with securing stay. Additional control stalk on right. Modified rear license plate mount. Coupe, DM 8690. Cabriolet, DM 9590.
1972:	6.00-15 tires, modified transmission ratios.
1973:	Modified details: interior sound insulation, nickel-plated muffler.
1974:	July, production ends.

Chapter 3

VW Type 147 (1964-74)

EA (Entwicklungsauftrag—development request) 149, the special car for the postal service. The first prototypes of the small van built by Westfalia were tested at the main office of the Freiburg postal service. The car was convincing, and mass production began in 1965.

At the beginning of the 1960s a vehicle appeared that was designed especially for postal workers and telephone repair personnel. It was to be used for transporting mail and packages in the city and in the country, in short, a vehicle for those cases where the Beetle was too small and the bus too big. The new small van, the Type 147 (nicknamed the "Fridolin") was the best of both worlds.

A mixture of Types 1, 2, and 3: Type 147. The vehicle was built until 1974, with Westfalia in Wiedenbrück building up to five per day.

The car with the amusing nickname was a car created for one of Volkswagen's largest customers, the German Postal Service. At the time, the German Postal Service had been using the 1957 Goggo TL250 for emptying mailboxes and for short trips. This van was almost three meters long, with sliding doors and could carry up to 300 kg. But the Goggo as well as the Lloyd LT 500 used before that was hopelessly underpowered and too small. Vans with an 1800-mm (TL 250) wheelbase were certainly not going to offer a lot of room inside. The VW, on the other hand, acted like an adult.

"So this is the vehicle that the newspaper *Bild* was calling a sensation; a vehicle that kept many people awake in anticipation. It's a harmless small van based on the VW 1200," stated *Motor-Rundschau* soberly in their 8/1965 issue. They included the first photographs of this almost 4-meter-long VW, whose life had begun as development request EA 149 in February 1962.

Volkswagen contracted with Westfalia in Wiedenbrück to develop and build this new workhorse for the postal service. Anything Westfalia was unable to build themselves was built by VW or Karmann. For example, Karmann in Osnabrück provided the platform from the Karmann-Ghia to be used as the base for the Type 147. VW's bus factory in Hanover provided many sheet metal parts such as both hood and rear engine cover. The front's resemblance to the VW 1500/Type 3 was unmistakable. The VW 1200 34 DIN hp engine was in the rear. The use of many parts from the VW parts bin made sense. It kept the cost of development down and also helped

Total length 3.97 m, curb weight 935 kg, and, thanks to the dual sliding doors as well as the rear door, incredibly practical: VW 147, 1966. Only a few of the vans were not delivered to the German postal service.

to speed up maintenance and repair for the postal service's garages. There were already almost 25,000 Volkswagens in the postal service's characteristic yellow driving around Germany. The fleet directors and mechanics were well acquainted with the cars that came out of Wolfsburg.

Westfalia presented the first two design sketches as well as a plastic model (1:8 scale) to the postal service in April 1962. The official presentation of the car was in January 1963 in Wiedenbrück. The car was worked on up to the last minute, which included lowering the roof by 9 cm the night before the presentation. The hard work paid off. Westfalia received an order for three Type 147 prototypes at the end of February and an order for five more later. The federal inspection service (TÜV) in Hanover passed prototypes 1 and 2. Number 1 remained at the Volkswagen factory for testing,

Model: Type 147
Built: 1965-74
Engine: 4-cylinder flat four, air-cooled
Valves: ohv, central camshaft
Displacement: 1192 cm^3
Bore x stroke: 77 x 64 mm
DIN horsepower (kW) @ rpm: 34 (25) @ 3600
Drive: rear wheels
Carburetion: one Solex 28 PICT
Transmission: 4 F, 1 R
Brakes: drums f/r
Top speed: 100 km/h
Curb weight: 935 kg
Tires: 5.60-15
Wheelbase: 2400 mm
Track f/r: 1305/1288 mm
L x W x H: 3970 x 1670 x 1730 mm

while number 2 was sent to the central technical center for the postal service in Darmstadt as a test and demo car.

During the IAA in September 1963, the main office of the Frankfurt postal service showed the prototype to heads of postal services from different countries. The "Fridolin" was well liked. Even if it looked a little odd with its 1.73-m high roof and sloping front end, the car was very practical. This was due in part to the 130-cm wide sliding doors and also the large van-like door in the rear used to fill the 81.2 ft^3 cargo area. A total of 400 kg could be loaded onto the van. The Fridolin's curb weight was 935 kg, around 200 kg heavier than the standard Beetle.

Mass production began in 1964 in Wiedenbrück. In the spring of 1965, Westfalia provided the press with a report including the many advantages of this new vehicle distributed by VW:

"The wide sliding doors open toward the rear and can be opened from the inside and locked from the outside. Each door has a sliding window. Both doors allow easy access to the cargo area and the driver's seat. The cargo area is also accessible through the rear door with window, that opens upward. When opened, the rear door can be locked into two positions. The door handle has a push-button. The driver's seat is mounted on a tube frame and can be slid back and forth. The seatback can be adjusted while driving. The seating position is designed to allow the driver to easily get out of the seat on both sides to reach the cargo area."

Private citizens could also buy the Fridolin (top speed: 100 km/h) for DM 6500. A foldable passenger seat was a DM 240 extra. There couldn't have been more than a handful of people who actually bought them. Of the 6139 Type 147 built, 85% went to the postal service; 1201 were sent to the Swiss postal service, albeit slightly modified. The Fridolin for the mountains of Switzerland had windows at the corners, a larger rear window and a parking heater. Production of the Type 147 ended in 1974 and the postal service began using basically standard two-door Golfs. The only similarity between the two vehicles was that they both only had two seats; the rear seats were removed, with a large cargo area painted yellow in its place.

Chapter 4

VW Type 181 (1969-78)

The Type 181 had a famous predecessor, the all-purpose car for the German troops during WWII, the VW Kübelwagen Type 82. The German commanders at the front loved it (Rommel was a Kübel fan) as did the Allies. US soldiers had a small manual explaining how to use the Kübelwagen and how to maintain it. No explanations or information were needed for the VW 181; at the end of the 1960s, every child knew how to work on a Beetle, there were over 5 million on the road in the US.

The predecessor of the "Kurierwagen" (VW 181) was the Kübelwagen from World War II, built at the VW factory, with some parts coming from Ambi-Budd in Berlin.

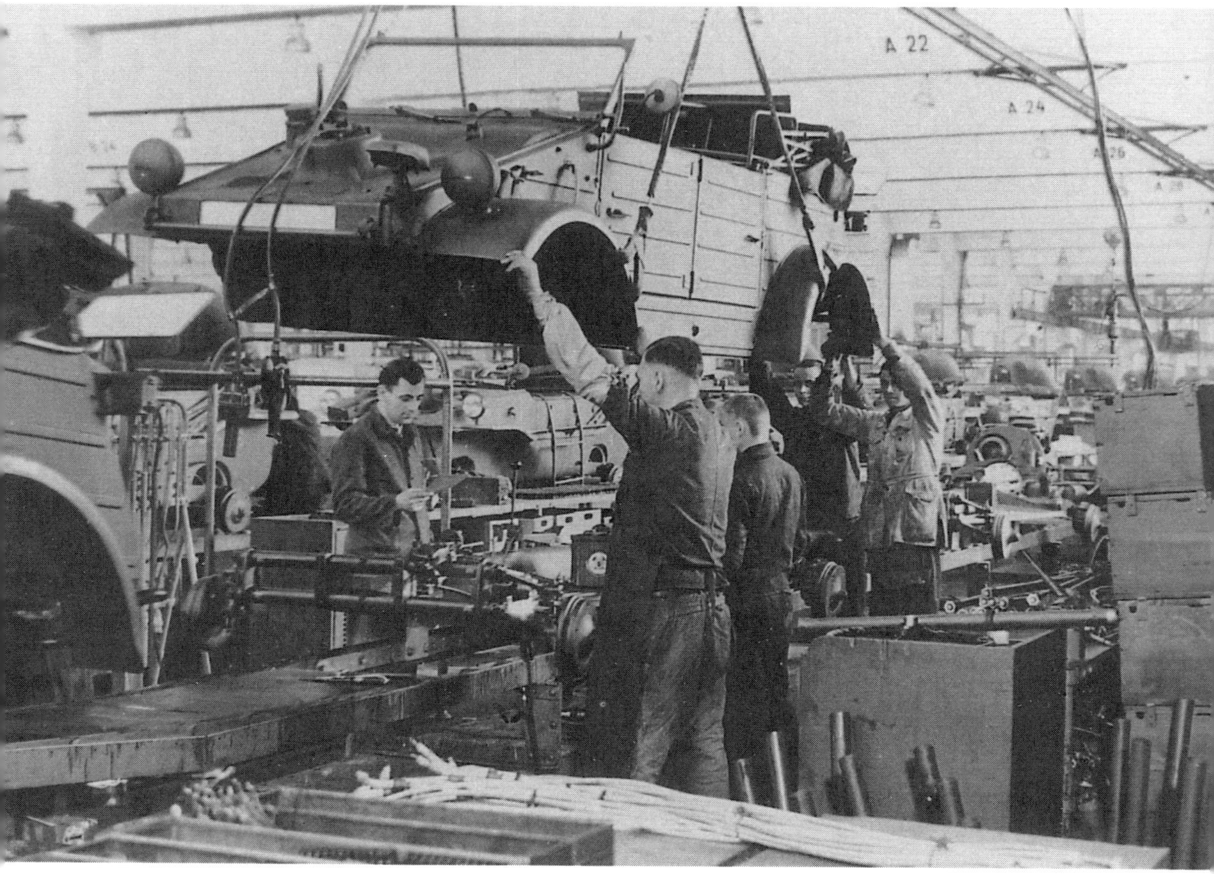

Model:
Type 181 Kurierwagen
Built: 1969-78
Engine: 4-cylinder, flat-four
Valves: ohv, central camshaft
Displacement: 1493 cm^3
Bore x stroke: 83 x 69 mm
DIN hp (kW) @ rpm:
44 (32) @ 4000 rpm
Drive: rear wheels
Carburetion:
one Solex 30 PICT-2
Transmission: 4F, 1R
Brakes: Drums f/r
Top speed: 115 km/h
Curb weight kg: 910
Tires: 165 SR 15 N
Wheelbase: 2400 mm
Track f/r: 1324/1436 mm
L x W x H:
3780 x 1640 x 1620 mm

The Design

The Body

The box-shaped body (this car had no curves) was bolted to the frame as on the Beetle, and reinforced at the front, sides and rear using wide metal ribbing. Only the rectangular windshield inside the wide frame was made of glass. The doors had plastic inserts that could be removed in seconds, packed into the included plastic cover and stored in the trunk. The windshield could be folded forward and locked into place on rubber snubbers.

The doors could be unhinged to allow easier access to the interior. If you drove around like this, the door cutouts had to be covered with a chain.

The lower side panels were quite high. This was done both to stiffen the body and allow the car to "wade" through water. With a total length of 3.78 m, this updated Kübel was almost 300 mm shorter than the Type 1, but it had four (albeit small) doors. The B pillar held the latch for the front door as well as the hinge for the rear door.

The instrument panel had the Beetle's instruments: speedometer, fuel gauge, and indicator lights for generator and oil pressure. A power outlet as well as a knob for the standard gasoline/electric heater were also included. The heater was located in the front storage area together with the spare tire and fuel tank. A cable allowed the hood to be unlatched from the inside, while the rear cover was opened from the outside using a push-button lock. The engine compartment was ventilated via side slits in the rear. The fuel filler cap was at the front right. The VW 181 did without sound insulation material or padded door trim. There was only bare metal to emphasize the fact that this car was built solely for utility. An open rubber mat covered the floor. Seats and seatbacks were covered in leatherette to be dirt-resistant and easy to clean.

Instead of a roof, the Type 181 had an uninsulated all-weather top covered with PVC that could be easily removed, rolled up and stored in the rear.

The Chassis

This Type 1 derivative used the floor pan from the Beetle, albeit the wider pan from the "smaller" Karmann-Ghia. The only changes to the floor pan were to install new mountings and additional reinforcements under the rear cross member. The front axle was similar to the Beetle's, with changes made to the steering knuckle and front axle supports. The rear swing axle was the one used in the old military Kübel and the first bus generation and provided around 20 cm of ground clearance. It also had equalizing springs on the rear axle. Steering and pedals were from the Beetle, as well as the front drum brakes. The rear 230-mm drums were from the bus. The five-hole steel wheels also came from the Type 2 and were equipped with 165 SR 14 M+S tires.

The Engine

The power plant was the 1500 four-cylinder flat-four engine from the Beetle. Displacement was 1.5 liters, and it output 44 DIN hp at 4400 rpm. Power transmission was via the fully synchronized four-speed from the Beetle, but with lower gearing. Larger changes were made for the 1971 model year, with the introduction of the 1.6-liter engine (same output but with reduced compression). This 50 DIN hp engine was also used in the VW 1302S.

VW 181 Kurierwagen

The Kübelwagen had many advantages for use in WWII, in spite of the fact that it did not have all-wheel drive. It had a high ground clearance, rear engine, and smooth floor pan, in addition to an adequately powered air-cooled engine and low weight (720 kg). The vehicle also offered a modicum of comfort, something a Jeep was not known for. In every army in the world, the commander usually sits in the back but not in the Jeep. The rear seat was so hard with inadequate springs that army leaders usually chose to sit in the passenger's seat.

Not a Kübelwagen, a Kurierwagen: The VW 181 could be used on easy to medium terrain, such as on this troop training area where this naval NCO is bringing food for the troops.

The VW 181 was to be built by Karmann, but in actuality rolled off the assembly line in Wolfsburg; between 1974 and 1975, 3654 units were built in the bus factory in Hanover to take advantage of unused capacity. After that, production was transferred to Mexico.

The new version of the Kübel was also not a true off-road vehicle; VW called it an "easy-access multi-purpose vehicle ," or a "Kurierwagen." The Americans just called it "The Thing."

The VW 181 was introduced to the public at the IAA in September 1969 and shortly thereafter in many barracks. The DKW-Jeep Munga was no longer built, and a successor was essential. The search for a successor was performed at many levels. The first company contracted to build a Euro Jeep was Hans Glas GmbH in Dingolfing, with the engine to come from MAN. A MAN engine was also at the heart of the FMS project, a joint effort between the NATO partners France, Italy, and Germany. But the cooperation between Fiat (Italy) and Saviem (France) was not successful; neither was the HBL all-wheel drive car project between Hotchkiss (France), Büssing (Germany), and Lancia (Italy). The only option left was the rear-wheel-drive Kübel.

The Type 181 is known as the child of Messrs. Nordhoff and Kessler; the latter worked in the federal defense ministry directing the team writing the specification book. The first order from the German army was for 2000 of these Spartan vehicles, which could also be purchased by civilians for DM 8500. This VW with the thick (more than 1 mm) metal panels used an amazing amount of fuel. *Auto, Motor und Sport* came up with 19.6 mpg, which when compared to the performance was quite a lot. Top speed for the 181 was 110 km/h according to the factory and could, under certain conditions, reach 115 km/h. At that speed, though, the car wasn't that much fun to drive. The 181 did without any sound-dampening

material or interior trim, which meant a loud drone that was particularly unbearable at 70 km/h with the top up. On the other hand, the low gearing made driving at lower speeds a lot of fun. The test teams had a lot of fun driving off at stop lights; the car hit 50 km/h in 6.5 seconds, something to be proud of. The 890-kg Kübel, on the other hand, didn't have a chance at 0-100 km/h, which took 36 seconds. But the VW 181 pulled strongly in second gear even at a crawl. The Kübel handled easy to medium terrain very well due to the high ground clearance and smooth underbody. On difficult terrain the Kübel drove as well or as poorly as a Beetle (or the wartime Type 82 Kübel). Even a rear-engine vehicle reaches its limits in extreme situations.

For DM 8500, a Type 181 with standard 44 DIN hp engine. For DM 9.99 (!) you could get the car in camouflage paint.

The stubnosed Beetle relative was reworked many times throughout its ten years of service, with the most important modifications done for the 1974 model year. These changes for the 48 DIN hp Kübel included wider tires (185 SR 14) and the semi-trailing link suspension from the 1302 and 1303. This made the 181 "one of the few off-road vehicles that can be driven well on regular roads," according to Clauspeter Becker in a 1976 report. This off-road specialist also felt that, "in spite of the average performance the vehicle drove much faster than many of its stronger competitors." The car was even better on off-road terrain thanks to the available limited-slip differential (DM 435). "As long as the ground is solid and rocky, the 181 can penetrate through even the most difficult ground.

The most important model changes and improvements VW 181:

1969: September, introduction of the VW 181 Kurierwagen. Open steel body, four doors, removable. Window inserts. Unpadded top, also removable. Foldable windshield; front defroster vents; warm air outlets in the footwell, passenger grab handle. Dual outside mirrors. Curb weight, 900 kg. Battery, 12-volt/36 Ah. Beetle mechanics. Frame from Karmann-Ghia Type 14. Engine, VW 1500. Chassis, Type 2 bus. Standard gasoline/electric heater. Top speed of 110 km/h. DM 8500.

Military package: multi-plate limited-slip differential.

1970: August, engine from the 1302S. Larger intake valves, larger oil pump gears. Modified cooling fan housing, aluminum oil cooler in bypass stream, larger cooling fan. Forked intake pipes, twin-port cylinder head, chrome-plated exhaust valves, different pistons. Carburetor 31 PICT, oil-bath air filter with thermostat, optional limited-slip differential (DM 435). Output, 44 DIN hp @ 3800 rpm; compression ratio, 6.6:1. Top speed, 115 km/h.

Padded dashboard, modified windshield mounting, trunk release moved to glove compartment. Control stalks from Type 3, diagnostic connector in engine compartment.

1971: March, final drive ratio 1.26 (previously 1.39), 5 JK x 14 wheels, 185 SR 14 tires. Track front/rear, 1354/1385 mm (previously, 1324/1346 mm).

1973: March, double-jointed rear axle with semi-trailing links, rear brakes from the Type 1302.

August, engine output increased to 48 DIN hp, compression ratio 7.3:1, transmission ratios changed. Control stalk with integrated wiper/washer switch from the Type 1. Four-spoke steering wheel with crash pad.

Export models: turn signals from the Type 13, exhaust emission control system and activated charcoal canister, different distributor, and altered fourth gear ratio.

1974: March, beach version designed "Acapulco," blue and white striped awning, similar pattern on seats, safety chains for driving with doors removed, running boards covered with rubber, lockable glove compartment, and Michelin 185 SR 14 tires. Never sold in Germany.

November, black air intake; previously, same as body color. Optional 24-volt electrical system (2 batteries, 2 generators, driven by second belt pulley on crankshaft).

Export models for North America: L-Jetronic engine, 50 DIN hp @ 4200 rpm. Paper air filter in plastic housing. 15,000 mile maintenance interval due to reinforced valve stems and smaller valve seats (30 mm instead of 32 mm).

1975: Production moved to Mexico.

1978: Production ends.

If the terrain is sandy, wet or muddy, the rear-wheel-drive isn't as helpful as the all-wheel-drive found in Jeeps."

VW had built 70,395 of the pseudo-off-road vehicles when production ended at the end of 1978. A low number of cars were built the last two years. The 181 was replaced by a true off-road vehicle, the VW Iltis, a car designed by Audi and built in much lower numbers. It was first built in Wolfsburg and later in Mexico.

Besides the army, other official agencies bought the VW 181, such as the post office's telephone service. The car was introduced in the US in 1973, resulting in the best year of production at 21,598 units.

Transporter predecessor: the Plattenwagen, based on sketches made by Ivan Hirst and built on the Type 1 platform. The last Plattenwagen was taken out of service in 1994.

Chapter 5

VW Type 2 (1950-90)

Pre-History

Professor Porsche had thought of converting a Volkswagen into a truck or van as early as the 1930s, but it was the British who actually made this a reality. When the heavy engineering unit left Wolfsburg in 1946 there were no more trucks within the factory. To fix this problem, Major Hirst had the Plattenwagen flat-bed built, which could be called the forerunner of the VW transporter. The last of these simple yet robust transport vehicles was taken out of service as late as 1994. The Plattenwagen had a ladder frame with Beetle axles and an open cab above the flat-four engine. Over the years engine output increased to a final 48 DIN hp in the last Plattenwagen, and the cab was covered and equipped with modern seats and headrests. But this was really still the vehicle that the

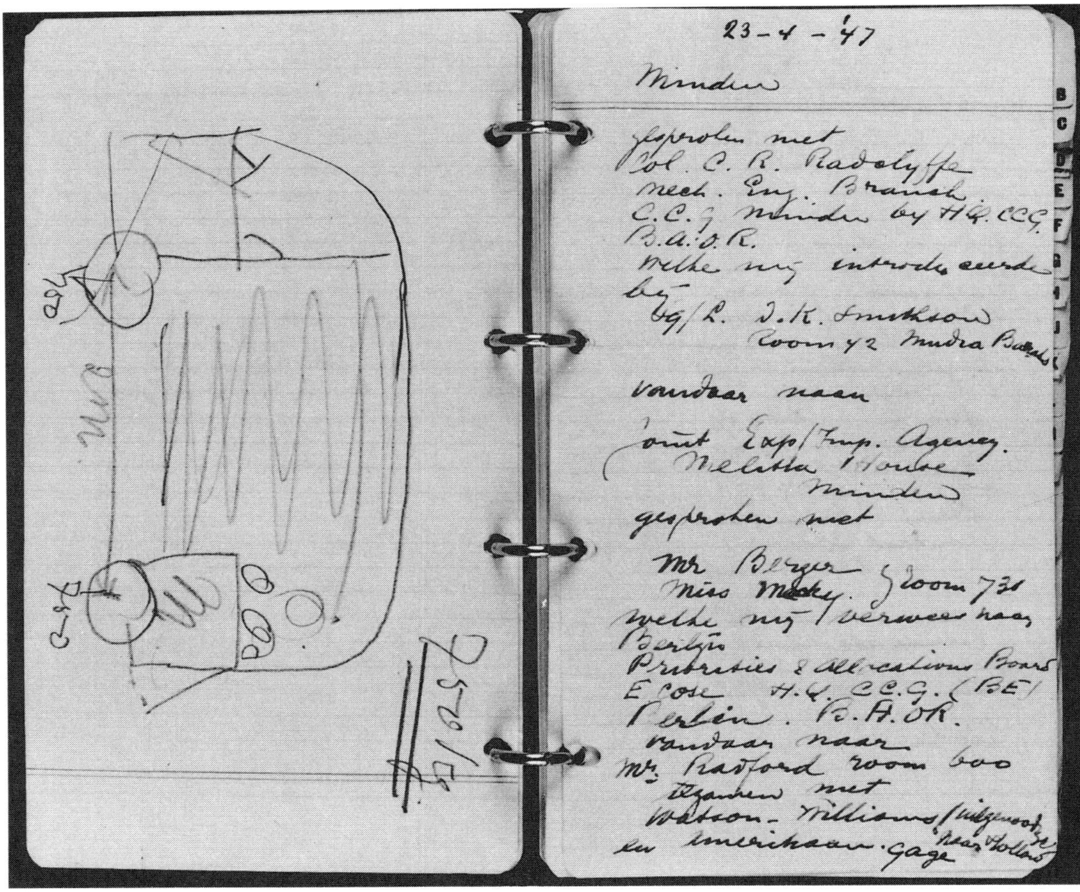

importer, Ben Pon, attempted to get street-legal certification for in the Netherlands. When this was rejected, he took his notebook and sketched a design for a van. Pon had been trying to become an importer of the KdF in the Netherlands since 1939. His design envisioned a van that could carry 750 kg, with a box-shaped body and rear engine/front steering.

VW development chief, Alfred Haesner, got the go ahead from Heinrich Nordhoff in the autumn of 1948 after taking a drive with him. In mid-November of the same year, Haesner asked for additional employees to work on the project. At that time, the first sketches and plans for the VW "Type 29" project had been drawn up. Heinrich Nordhoff looked at them for the first time on November 20, 1948. Version A had a flat, straight driver cab. Version B had a front that was slightly raked without a projecting roof. Nordhoff gave his approval for version B. Various individual parts were tested in parallel to the display model, in particular shock absorbers and torsion bars.

Ben Pon, the Dutch VW importer, saw a Plattenwagen while touring the factory in 1947 and sketched his idea of the Transporter in his notebook. His ideas were the impetus behind the development of the Transporter.

Above: The preproduction car "Number 4." The first prototype built in 1949 used the chassis from the Beetle. To meet the higher demands of the Transporter, VW had to develop a unitized body.

The first car was ready on March 11; the first prototype tests took place on April 5 and were quickly finished: the Beetle chassis was not strong enough to withstand the significantly higher stresses. Alfred Haesner's men began to build a unitized body that was to be stiffer as well as lighter. The only similarity between prototype 2 and the Beetle was the engine. The new design was able to withstand the rigors of the test drive over the worst roads in Lower Saxony (starting at the factory, through Warmenau, Wittlingen, Hankensbüttel, Luttern and Gifhorn, and back to Wolfsburg) without any major problems. Besides the comprehensive 12,000-km test drive, the VW testers had also wanted to test the vehicle on a hill at the north curve on the Nürburgring; they were unable to do this due to a lack of time.

On May 19, 1949, Heinrich Nordhoff set the start of production date: November 1. The absolute latest date to start was December 1, 1949, in order to be able to deliver cars by the beginning of 1950.

The first Transporter from 1953. Production of the van started in March, followed by the Kombi in May (which was available with or without seat benches). The bus completed the family in June 1950 in seven-, eight-, and nine-seater variants.

Transporter production began with a capacity of 10 units per day. A Type 2 cost DM 5850 — DM 1050 more expensive than the sedan but cheaper than the Cabriolet.

A look into the prototype's engine compartment. The engine was the 1.1-liter four-cylinder from the Beetle, installed in the rear. It output 25 DIN hp @ 3300 rpm. The fuel tank is on the left, the spare tire on the right. For production, Heinrich Nordhoff relocated the spare tire to above the engine.

The Design

The Engine

The engine was the well-known four-cylinder flat four engine from the Beetle, including a single Solex downdraft carburetor with throttle and choke. The oil-bath air filter, as usual, sat on top of the carburetor. In the pickup and ambulance, it was located on the left of the engine. Displacement and output were the same as for the Beetle, as were the gear ratios and differential reduction ratio.

The 41-liter fuel tank with three-way fuel tap and reserve switch sat on the top of the engine in the engine compartment in the van and bus. Any overflowing fuel when filling up was caught by the plate above the engine. In the pickup and ambulance, the tank was located in a separate compartment in front of the engine compartment underneath the cargo area. Only the van got the auxiliary 1:1.4 reduction gear on both rear wheels. This was something that had been used in the old military Kübelwagen and improved hill-climbing ability. The factory set top speed at 80 km/h and put a sticker on the windshield to inform the driver of this. The van could be driven much faster, though, without any fear of damaging the engine.

The Chassis

The van was of unitized construction, supported by a reinforcement frame attached to the floor pan. The latter consisted of two longitudinal members connected by two welded transverse members.

Two to three people fit on the bench with adjustable seatback.

Convincing: The ability to carry three-quarters of a metric ton in 162 ft^3 gave the Type 2 a market share of over 30% four years after its introduction. The picture shows a van from 1952, which can be identified by the upper air inlets.

Nimble: 11-m turning circle, only two turns of the wheel from lock to lock. This shows an ambulance's cockpit from 1954. The sticker on the window indicates the 30 DIN hp engine, used since January 1954.

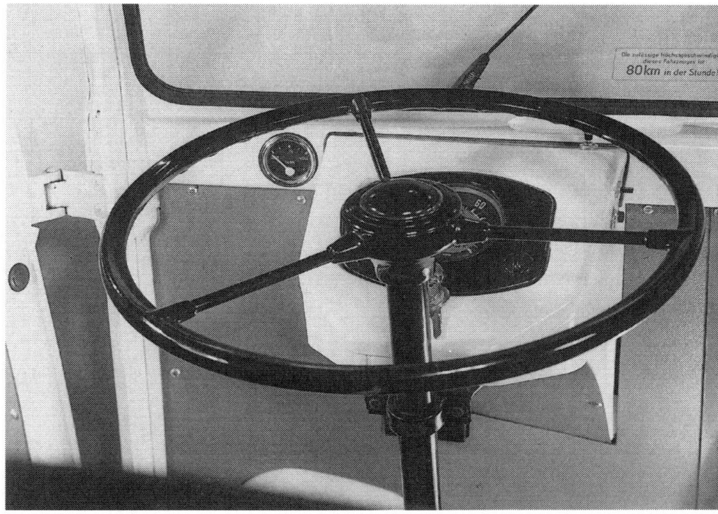

In the spring of 1955 fresh-air ventilation became standard in the Transporter. The air intake was in the roof overhang above the windshield. This cutaway illustrates the new location of the spare tire and fuel tank, now both outside the engine compartment to increase cargo area.

The front axle was another inheritance from the Beetle, albeit modified. In the bus, Kombi, and pickup, the top torsion bar was four-leaf, the lower, three-leaf. The rear swing-arm axle was basically the same one used in the Beetle except that the drive shafts terminated in reduction gears (which caused some problems when driving). Braking was via a simplex brake system with front and rear 230-mm drums. The effective brake area was larger than the Beetle's, however. The van rode on 16-inch steel wheels with a 3.5-inch offset and 5.50-16 tires. The spare tire for the bus, Kombi and eight-seater was located in the engine compartment; in the pickup and ambulance it was behind the seatback in the cab.

The Body

According to the technical data provided by the factory, the new cab-forward design was an "airplane-type design (lightweight)" with "unitized, stiff all-steel box body (with no separate chassis) with one-piece all-steel roof; a streamlined form with a low Cd value of 0.44; the load area was between the axles."

Channel sections took care of the stability of the windows and door frames while the outer walls were reinforced using box members. The floor and interior walls were reinforced by heavy ribbing and supported by transverse members; only the driver's door could be locked (the passenger door locked from the inside).

Transporter bodies-in-white in the Wolfsburg factory, 1953. The pickup was added to the bus, van, and Kombi Transporter family in September 1952. This was an excellent idea considering the post-war construction boom at the time.

The two- to three-seat bench sat above the front axle on the wheel wells. The tool kit was located beneath this. The split-screen windshield with centerpiece was slightly angled. An optional opening windshield was available at extra cost and were often ordered with the special edition. It could be tilted outward to a horizontal position and held in place by two wing nuts. The windshield wipers first had to be moved and hooked into special brackets. The van got front side-vent windows even before the Beetle. As the literature of the day stated, these had a "lock tab and a secure handle with push button to prevent theft."

Cargo area ventilation in the bus was via side inlets in the extra cargo area. Roof ventilation was available at extra cost starting in 1953; the air flowed in just above the windshield and was collected in the interior air scoop between the bulkhead and the cargo area. Corresponding air inlets were located in the front and on the side and flaps were used to regulate airflow through them. An optional electric fan increased airflow but also caused roof area around the air outlet to be dirtied quickly. Heating, as in the Beetle, was by air warmed by the engine, controlled by a rotary knob beside the driver's seat. As in the Beetle, there was a 6-volt electrical system with an 84Ah battery installed on the right side of the engine compartment.

The individual models within the bus family were differentiated mainly by window placement and equipment installed. The van, Kombi and bus all had a single-piece roof, a two-part side door as well as a steel floor pan. Whereas the bulkhead between the cargo area and cab only went halfway up in the bus and Kombi, it went all the way to the roof in the van. There was a small window in the fiberboard for a rear view.

The list of available options was quite comprehensive even then, and it grew during the 1950s. The rear door could be ordered with or without windows. All models could be ordered with opening windshields; the eight-seater, Kombi and ambulance could also be ordered with six quarter vents in the passenger compartment.

The dashboard on all models was fairly simple, with a small instrument panel in front of the driver as well as semaphore indicator switch. The upper instrument panel insert was made of pressed material. The starter button was located to the left of the steering wheel. The speedometer was only 100 mm in diameter with a trip odometer as well as high beam, generator, oil pressure, and semaphore indicator lights. There were also two rotary knobs for lighting and the windshield wipers, as well as the ignition switch. The low-beam switch was on the floor to the left of the clutch. A switch on the dashboard activated the semaphore indicators. There was also a power outlet for an inspection lamp.

Bare metal dominated the rear cargo area. Both the van and the Kombi did without interior trim. The bus and the "Samba" special

The boss speaks: The 100,000th Transporter came off the assembly line on October 9, 1954. That year, VW built a total of 40,199 Transporters, with an average of 153 per workday.

model did a little bit better. The dashboard stretched across the vehicle but was not much better equipped than in the other models. It did have a clock and an ashtray, and there was a place for a radio in front of the passenger seat—a wide dashboard was only available for the bus at extra cost. These models seemed a little more liveable with a floor covered by a rubber mat. All Type 2s had a rubber mat in the cab. Mats in the passenger compartment were standard in the Transporter and extra cost in the other models.The bulkhead was covered in hardboard, with leatherette on top of that. All models had door trim made of hardboard; in the luxury version, this was covered

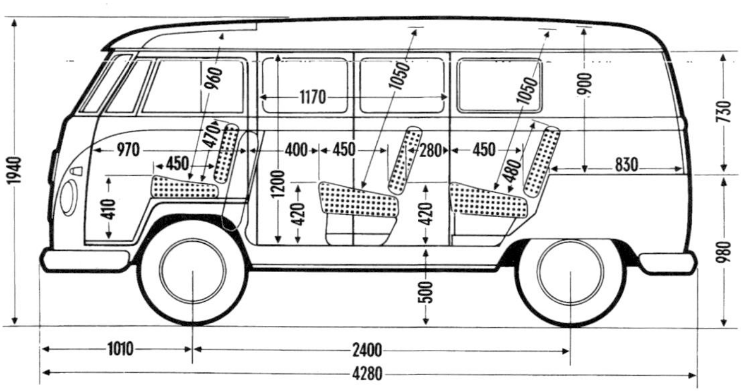

Excellent use of space: a first-generation Type 2 bus.

with leatherette. The luxury models did without the passenger grab handle on the dashboard. Footrests were installed in all models.

The cargo area in the van was used as a passenger area in the bus and the special model. VW engineers installed two upholstered, three-seat benches that could be easily removed. The front bench was a split and foldable design. A Golde sliding sunroof was standard in the eight-seater special model but cost extra in the bus or Kombi.

The eight-seater and the Kombi had three windows on each side. Those in the rear could be opened outward. The Samba bus, officially known as the "eight-seater special model" by VW, had an additional side window in the cargo area as well as rear corner windows made of 4-mm plexiglas. The characteristic roof glazing and four small lights on either side were reserved for the special edition.

The Samba model included an ashtray, headliner, grab handles, armrests on the side, clothes hooks and an assist strap in the rear. It also came with a standard rearview mirror and passenger sun visor starting in 1961, which both cost extra in the bus. The cargo area above the engine in the bus was trimmed in hardboard, with loop-pile carpeting in the special edition. Only the Samba had metal protective trim, with a rail in the special edition.

Only the bus were available with two-tone paint from the factory, wide rear rubber covered bumper (it reached around the side of the Transporter and was available from 1953), wide aluminum trim and chrome-plated 315-mm VW logo. The latter was in body color in the other models.

Below left:
Tasteful, the interior of the bus. Since March 1955, the spare tire was no longer located in the engine compartment of the bus and van. It was now located in an area behind the front seat.

Below right:
A 1955 Samba. The special luxury version of the bus with a lot of chrome and even more windows was introduced in April 1951. The luxury Samba bus had a standard 23 windows and a folding sunroof.

VW Transporter Type 2/T1 (1950-67)

Model: Type 2/T1 Van
Built: 1950-53
Engine: 4-cylinder, flat-four
Valves: ohv, central camshaft
Displacement: 1131 cm^3
Bore x stroke: 75 x 64 mm
DIN hp (kW) @ rpm: 25 (18) @ 3300
Drive: rear wheels
Carburetion: 26 VFIS; from Oct. 1, 1952, one Solex 28 PCI
Transmission: 4F, 1R
Brakes: drums f/r
Top speed: 85 km/h
Curb weight: 975 kg
Tires: 6.40 - 15 6PR
Wheelbase: 2400 mm
Track f/r: 1370/1375 mm
L x W x H: 4280 x 1800 x 1925 mm

At a press conference on November 12, 1949, Heinrich Nordhoff introduced the first-generation Transporter to the public. The engineers and designers called it a "combination of a unitized body with the main characteristics of a Volkswagen." The form had been designed with "modern tendencies," looking at Auto Union's DKW delivery truck which had been announced in August 1949 and available two months later in October. That truck could carry three-quarters of a metric ton. It had a two-cylinder, two-stroke engine (with 20 DIN hp at first) installed in the front and easily accessible. In addition, the DKW was less than 4 m long and had an amazing 148 ft^3 cargo area. VW, though, had also done their homework. Their vehicle had a 162 ft^3 cargo area and was 4.15 m long (1.66-m width, 1.9-m height). VW's well-known 1.1-liter flat-four was installed in the rear and output 25 DIN hp @ 3300 rpm. The new Transporter from Wolfsburg also had a low weight of 975 kg (curb weight with full tank, tool kit, spare tire, driver and passenger) and could carry 750 kg. The maximum gross weight was 1725 kg. The VW's performance and economy was a definite plus over the competition from DKW and Company. The VW got 25 mpg, according to the owner's manual, which meant a full tank could take you 500 km.

The first vehicles came off the assembly line in February 1950. Actual mass production began in March with ten vehicles built daily.

From 1959 the bus had a modified engine with the same output as before (30 DIN hp) but increased torque. For the first time, the four-speed transmission was fully synchronized. From June 1960 the bus had the larger export bumper as well as the turn signals installed in place of the antiquated semaphore indicators.

Left: The beloved Microbus from the 1950s was a Type 2. This picture shows the special model from 1959. In August of that year, VW celebrated over 500,000 Type 2s sold.

At first the Transporter was only available as a van at a cost of DM 5850 (not much more expensive than the Beetle, with which it had a lot in common). The van (Type 21) was soon followed by a number of other commercial vehicles. The Kombi (Type 23) was introduced in May 1950, only a month after production began. The Type 23 came with two benches for transporting passengers. The true Microbus (Type 22) was introduced in June 1950. It was fairly identical to the Kombi, but it was better equipped. A foldable cloth sunroof was available for this model as well as a rear door. By the end of that year, daily production had risen from 10 to 60; the first year there were more Transporters in circulation than the competition's vehicles. A luxury version followed in June 1951. This was the Samba bus (special model Type 24).

The cooperative project with the German Red Cross was relatively down-to-earth. The VW ambulance (Type 27) was introduced in December 1951. In 1950-1, Miesen Company converted some Kombis to ambulances on their own. The pickup (Type 26) came in August 1952 with its corrugated steel floor and hardwood trim. The sides could be flipped up. Beneath the bed was an additional cargo area. The fuel tank was directly above the rear axle with the filler cap on the side. To save space, the spare tire was located behind the bench. This arrangement was used in the other Transporter models starting in 1955. The optional pickup was available with tonneau cover and bows at extra cost.

There was a Transporter for every situation. This is a low-loader from 1962, a pickup with swinging doors and additional frame reinforcements.

The bus and Kombi were identical in construction. The Kombi had removable benches resulting in a van with windows. Another difference between the Kombi and the bus (besides the roof glazing): the Microbus could be used as a passenger car as it was available as a seven-, eight-, or nine-seater. Heinz Kranz from the magazine *Das Automobil* tested the eight-seater (DM 8475) in their September 1957 issue. Kranz, the senior editor, took the van to Lake Garda in Italy. His conclusion: body and engine were above average and "bore little relation to the pure technical data." He also was amazed by the handling ("safe for any driver"), the amount of space ("exemplary"), and the equipment level ("when one examines the interior one isn't sure whether to be amazed by the luxury or the amount of space"). But he did have some negative comments: "The windshield could be improved by being just one piece, not two, or the rearview mirror should be moved," or "As much as I was excited about the improvements made to the rear window, I still can't understand why a fuel gauge is not standard." Besides these comments, he had only praise for the VW: "The bus and the Transporter in general are OK in every respect. It was no surprise that I encountered 30 VW special model buses between the Brenner Pass and Trient with 200 people heading for rest and relaxation. The bus offers everything a vehicle owner or passenger could want."

Ten years later (*Das Automobil* had been discontinued at the beginning of the 1960s) *Mot* tested the VW Transporter and came up with different results. They tested it against the Ford Transit, the VW's strongest rival, and the Hanomag F20. "In terms of price and maintenance, the VW is well worth it. Handling and use of space,

Model: Type 2/T1 Kombi
Built: 1962-67
Engine: 4-cylinder, flat-four
Valves: ohv, central camshaft
Displacement: 1493 cm^3
Bore x stroke: 83 x 69 mm
DIN hp (kW) @ rpm:
42 (29) @ 4000
Drive: rear wheels
Carburetion:
one Solex 28 PICT-1; from 1965, 30 PICT-1
Transmission: 4F, 1R
Brakes: drums f/r
Top speed: 105 km/h
Curb weight kg: 1140
Tires: 7.00 - 14 6PR
Wheelbase: 2400 mm
Track f/r: 1375/1360 mm
L x W x H:
4280 x 1750 x 1925 mm

however, are a few steps behind the Ford Transit. The Ford has the most to offer relative to the price with its good handling and suspension, quiet engine, practical standard equipment and large cargo area behind the seats."

The buyers, though, had the final word: The Transporter factory in Hanover pumped out 750 units per day (a total of 176,275 in 1966 with a market share of 79%). Ford's Genk factory produced 220 units a day, and Hanomag manufactured 55 of their vehicles a day in their Hamburg-Harburg plant. This relationship didn't change much, especially since the second-generation Transporter was already in the works at VW.

VW Transporter/Bus T2 (1967-79)

The Transporter got a facelift after the factory vacation in 1967 and 17 years of production with around 1.8 million built. Preparations and planning for the new Type 2 had begun in 1964. The design department under Gustav Mayer had their hands full making sure they were within the tight deadlines set by Heinrich Nordhoff. They created a modern design with very wide windows, redesigned front, single curved windshield, and air inlets in the D pillar; the vehicle known internally as the T2 was significantly different from the T1. Gustav Mayer didn't just perform a facelift but built a

Food on wheels: A VW Transporter with Westfalia conversion as a baker's van.

The most important model changes and improvements Transporter T1:

1949: November, introduction of the Transporter.

1950: March, production of Type 2 Transporter begins. At first only van in blue available, DM 5850. Van with wing doors opening to the side.

June, Kombi production starts (DM 6350). Nine-seater bus (DM 6650). Bus available with rear hatch and folding sunroof. Automatic cooling regulation via thermostat.

1951: January, suspension modified, crankcase made of magnesium alloy.

March, clutch cable moved, fibre cam gear.

April, special edition Samba bus: glazing all around, skylights on side, two-tone paint, special interior with headliner, side trim, and chrome trim.

June, mass production of Samba bus begins, official designation: eight-seater "special model."

All models: Modified heat exchangers and heater control cable, wheel housing covered in felt. Transporter: with rear window. Van: with rear window and window in wall separating cargo area from passenger area.

1952: January, special ambulance edition introduced.

September, Van now standard model. Production of pickup starts.

All models: Steering damper with stronger spring, larger taillights. Now only one valve spring.

1953: January, engine modifications, modified final drive ratio. Modified hand brake lever. Crank windows instead of quarter vents.

March, 2nd, 3rd and 4th gears synchronized.

October, 160-watt generator.

1954: 30 DIN hp engine introduced with 1192 cm^3 displacement. Speedometer now indicates 100 km/h. 3rd and 4th gears modified, combined ignition/starter installed, as well as improved seat springs. Flat-top pistons used, compression now 6.6:1 (previously 6.1).

December, rear bumper standard for all models.

1955: March, windshield 15 mm taller, roof extends beyond body, fresh-air intake above windshield. Larger rear window and hatch. Fuel tank located above rear axle (previously in engine compartment), tank filler cap on right in front of air inlets. Modified cooling fan, oil-bath air filter on side of engine. Spare tire moved to front behind cab wall. Cargo area above engine compartment lowered 30 cm, cargo area now 170 ft^3 (previously 162 ft^3), 15" tires instead of 16" 6.40-15 tires. Modified front and rear track as well as brake system (drums, master cylinder). Dual-circuit brakes in front, single in rear. Modified front suspension (softer springs, rearranged links). Telescopic shock absorbers in rear. Telescopic steering dampers.

All models: Dashboard extends across entire width of vehicle, larger speedometer. Two-spoke steering wheel. Gas pedal instead of roller. Fuel lever in front underneath driver seat. Improved seat padding. Front axle load 950 kg, rear 1000 kg, GVWR 1.85 metric tons (Transporter).

1956: March, production in Hanover factory begins. Standard right outside mirror. Bus and special model available as seven-seater.

1957: Modified clutch, magnetic oil drain plug. IAA: Double cab introduced, large-capacity pickup (Westfalia), box-van and pickup with dolly.

1958: November, production of double cab, large-capacity pickup and police emergency vehicle begins. All models: stronger bumpers, underbody painted. Different taillights, safety glass windshield. Different gear ratios for 3rd and 4th gears. Fuel pump with larger capacity.

VW Westfalia camper introduced.

1959: May, engine modifications: stronger crankshaft, larger crankcase, angled valves. Output: 30 DIN hp, torque 78 Nm @ 2000 rpm. Fully synchronized four-speed transmission, cooling fan reduction gear ratio 1:1.8 (previously 1.2).

Autumn, improved heating, reinforced front axle, and 180-watt generator. Hand brake lever moved forward.

1960: March, turn signals instead of semaphore indicators.

July, three-way adjustable seatback, plug-in connectors for electrics, asymmetric low beams.

August, 28 PICT carburetor with automatic choke, pre-heated air filter, compression ratio to 7.1:1. 34 DIN hp @ 3600 rpm, torque 82 Nm @ 2000 rpm. Larger brake cylinder, GVWR 1.865 metric tons.

October, three-way adjustable seatback.

1961: Presentation of van with high roof at IAA.

August, maintenance-free tie rods, steering linkage, pedals and hand brake cable. New steering damper mounting. Steering ignition lock standard. New shift linkage, different transmission ratios. Crankcase ventilation in air filter, fuel gauge instead of fuel lever, passenger sun visor and grab handle. Two-chamber taillights.

1962: January, US models available with mounting points for seatbelts.

August, bucket seat for driver with foldable seatback. Larger wheel cutouts. Shallower headlight pods, deeper spare tire well. Improved valve train, new intake manifold, stronger cooling fan, larger clutch diameter. Pickup: spare tire located under truck bed.

October, VW Transporter 1500 introduced, output 42 DIN hp @ 3800 rpm, top speed of 105 km/h @ 3630 rpm. 28 PICT-1 carburetor with improved automatic choke. Max. uphill grade 28% (previously 26%).

1963: Type 2 available with 1.5-liter engine and 42 DIN hp. Upright fan.

January, all models: fresh-air heating with separate pipework for heat and cooling air from fan.

March, type 2/1500 available for delivery, larger brake drum diameter, reinforced front axle, steering knuckle and shock absorbers. More powerful generator, modified final drive ratio (4.125 instead of 4.43). Auxiliary reduction ratio of 1.26, previously 1.39.

May, sliding door for van and bus (M package, DM 250).

	August, crankcase ventilation with water separator as in the VW Beetle, larger brakes for all Transporters, progressive rubber stops between the trailing links on front axle. Larger rear hatch (except for van and ambulance). Larger flat front turn signals (as used in US models).
	Special editions: Rear round corner window dropped. Right outside mirror. Flexible knobs instead of coat hooks. Eight-seater dropped.
	VW 1500 Transporter with 1.0 metric ton capacity introduced: 7.00-14 tires on 5J x 14 wheels. Reinforced axles, auxiliary springs in the rear. Complete program: 0.8 metric ton capacity 1200/1500 for bus, special edition, van, Kombi, pickup, and ambulance; 1.0 metric ton capacity 1500 for Kombi, van, pickup, and fire truck.
1964:	January, all models now with tubeless 7.00-14 tires. Ambulance: larger rear hatch.
	July, 0.8 metric ton /1200 only available as option. New cooling air regulation with flaps instead of throttle ring, improved heating actuation. Standard engine speed limiter (previously part of M package). Windshield wipers park automatically, larger wiper area. Transmission modifications. Modified final drive bearing and rear axle joints. Windshield washers, rearview mirror. Bus: plastic headliner.
1965:	44 DIN hp, 30 PICT-1 carburetor with engine speed limiter. Torsion bar stabilizer on front axle, new shock absorbers. Low- to high-beam switch on control stalk, high-beam signal, two-speed wipers.
1966:	12-volt electrical system, new Drehfallen door locks, lower 3rd gear ratio.

Undivided enthusiasm: After 17 years of production with around 1.8 million built, the second Transporter generation was introduced in 1967 after the factory vacation—with a one-piece windshield.

roomier and stiffer body. The wheelbase remained the same at 2400 mm, but the second-generation Transporter was 160 mm longer at 4420 mm. The length increased the front and rear overhangs by 100 mm. Width remained approximately the same (around 1770 mm).

The usable interior space was enlarged due in part to the increase in length but also to a lowered floor. This was due in turn to the new double joint rear axle with semi-trailing links, which replaced the old axle taken from the military Kübelwagen. The front axle remained basically unchanged, with less bearing maintenance required. A standard dual-circuit brake system was used. The engine was the 1.6-liter with 47 DIN hp @ 4000 rpm used in the Type 3. Maximum torque was 103 Nm @ 2200 rpm. The transmission with long shift lever also came from the sedan. The only difference was a different 4th gear ratio. Wolfsburg engineers had modi-

Left:
The last major visible model improvements were in August 1963. Type 2 models built after that had a larger rear hatch with chrome Transporter insignia. Nothing more changed up to the end of the 1967 model year; after that, the tank cover, grab handle under rear door, air vent, and so on changed.

Beautiful living: Bucket seats with access to cargo area. Compared to the T1 the dashboard is full of equipment, with a large compartment on the passenger side, and armrests on the doors with air vents below them.

fied the engine mounts to reduce engine noise for the passengers. This is at least what the factory information said. Testers at the time felt differently about this: the noise at "high engine speeds got on their nerves." The only way to reduce the noise was to fill the trunk, which was fairly easy to do considering the large hatch and the opening was lowered by 73 mm. Access to the cargo and passenger area was also much easier due to the 1050-mm-wide sliding door on the side. A sliding door on the other side was an available option.

The model line itself hadn't changed that much. There was still the van, pickup, Kombi, and bus, as well as the eight-seater special edition, which was at first known as the Clipper L in the model list. The Clipper L name turned out to be a problem when the US airline Pan Am sued VW as they had already copyrighted that name. This may not have interested Germans, but it was a big deal in the US where VW sold the most luxury buses. The importance of the US market was noted right at the beginning of the Clipper test in the October 1967 issue of *Motor Rundschau*: "It was 'a standard thing' for the father of a swarm of children to buy the 'Microbus'." This hadn't become "as popular in Germany yet," but it must be recognized that "this bus is much more sensible than many of the passenger cars available."

In January 1955 it was decided to give the Transporter its own factory. A factory was built in Hanover-Stöcken. The first Transporter came off the assembly line there on March 8, 1965, exactly six years after the first Transporter was built in Wolfsburg; it was a pickup. This picture is from 1967; the large turn signals (at first only installed in US models) had been standard since August 1963.

VW first offered an alternative to the 1.6-liter flat-four engine for the 1971 model year. The 1.7-liter flat engine had been tested in the VW 411 and was space-saving due to the relocated cooling fan. The engine output 66 DIN hp @ 4900 rpm. Photo shows a 2.0 liter engine.

Well-deserved praise: "In terms of driving and suspension, handling, comfort, and space available, the new Transporter can hardly be recognized as the successor to the previous Transporter," according to Richard Köbberling in the 12/67 issue of *lastauto omnibus*. This praise was due largely to the chassis with front and rear independent suspension.

After reading the test, readers could only agree; a VW had again passed the exam with honors. Testers spoke of a "chassis typical of a passenger car" that even forgave major mistakes and of the "excellent build quality." The one exception that reduced the marks somewhat was the driver's poor seating position due to the vertical seatback and insufficient thigh support.

That "enthusiastic but loud" engine was very thirsty considering its average performance was also one of the more negative points. The engine got 20 mpg, and at a constant full throttle this was reduced to 18 mpg. Top speed was a fairly low 114 km/h even if the speedometer read 140 km/h or more when driving downhill.

For advertising purposes: The first second-generation Transporters were driven under their own power to the dealers. This picture shows a group of cars leaving the factory in Hanover-Stöcken with temporary plates and stickers that say "Der neue VW Transporter" (The New VW Transporter).

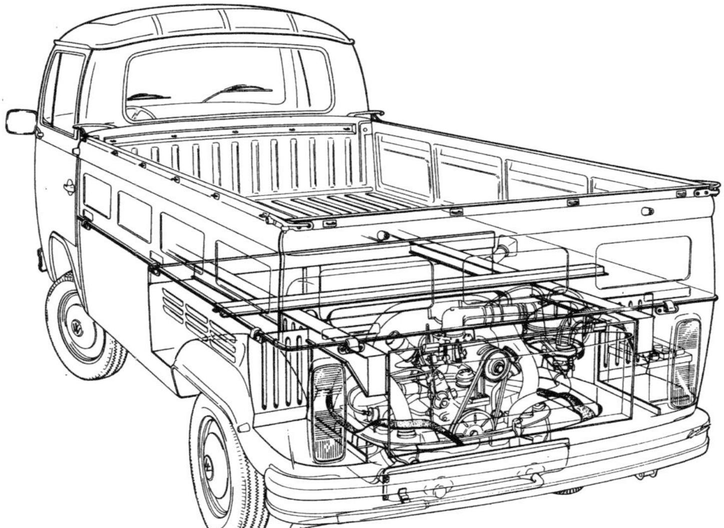

From the beginning, VW offered a wide range of different Transporter models. This shows a cutaway of the pickup from 8/72.

Quiet entrance: This unique pickup from 1972 had an electric motor (the only one ever built).

Model: Type 2/T2 Kombi
Built: 1967-70
Engine: 4-cylinder, flat-four
Valves: ohv, central camshaft
Displacement: 1584 cm³
Bore x stroke: 85.5 x 69 mm
DIN hp (kW) @ rpm:
47 (34) @ 4000
Drive: rear wheels
Carburetion:
one Solex 30 PCIT-2
Transmission: 4F, 1R
Brakes: drums f/r
Top speed: 105 km/h
Curb weight: 1140 kg
Tires: 7.00-14 6PR/8PR
Wheelbase: 2400 mm
Track f/r: 1385/1426 mm
L x W x H:
4420 x 1765 x 1940 mm

Engine performance continued to be important. For the 1971 model year, VW installed a cylinder head with dual inlet ports, bringing output up to 50 DIN hp @ 4000 rpm. The next year, the 1.7-liter flat engine was available as an option (flat because the cooling fan was now installed on the crankshaft to save space). For the 1974 model year, the 66 DIN hp power plant from the Type 4 gave way, as in the sedan, to the 1.8-liter with 68 DIN hp. A 2-liter engine was available starting in 1976. This engine was also installed in the VW Porsche 914. The output of the Transporter engine increased from 30 to 70 DIN hp with a Solex double carburetor used instead of fuel injection. The maximum torque of 140 Nm was now available at 2800 rpm. The new engine was very convincing to the testers, such as Clauspeter Becker who wrote in the 21/1976 issue of *Auto, Motor und Sport* that the "power bus" now had enough power "for very rapid acceleration in traffic." Becker also came to the same conclusion his colleague from *Motor Rundschau* had nine years before: the bus was anything but economical when it came to fuel. At 110 km/h the bus only got 17 mpg; at a constant full throttle this was easily reduced to 16 mpg. During the test, the bus went up to 133 km/h.

When introduced, the normal eight-seater Clipper cost DM 7980; the L model with "2 sun visors, windshield washers, clock, heating and belted radials" cost DM 8980. The recommended parking heater cost DM 350 extra, while a steel sunroof added DM 450 to the price.

No luck with names: Originally the second-generation bus was to be called the "Clipper," but the name had to be changed for legal reasons. There was no successor to the Samba bus with roof glazing. The new special model was just called "Eight-seater L" and had a crank steel sunroof instead of the folding sunroof.

The large taillights were a sign of the Transporter built after the factory vacation in 1971. In September of that year, the three millionth VW Transporter left the factory. This Transporter factory now had the largest number of workers it had ever had: 28,728 people were on the payroll. The photo shows a Type 26 built after August 1972.

Crisis: While the Transporter was getting better and better (this picture shows a van from the 1973 model year), German industry was falling deeper into the oil crisis. The drop in exports and the transfer of engine production to Salzgitter meant a large number of layoffs. At the end of 1975, only 16,867 people worked at the factory in Hanover.

Prices were an important topic in the 1976 test. Even the bus with L package at DM 17,350 didn't come standard with "such obvious items as a rear window defroster, reverse lights, safety glass, automatic seatbelts, a padded dash, day/night rearview mirror or locks for the fuel tank or engine cover," to say nothing of other extras such as a sunroof (DM 735) or parking heater (DM 1031). "It is therefore not difficult at all to end up with a price for a VW Bus or Kombi much higher than DM 20,000."

VW Transporter T3 (1979-90)

Anybody who though the engine in the new Transporter was going to move to the front as in many other vehicles of the time was disappointed: the Transporter remained a rear engine vehicle. That wasn't what the designers working with Gustav Mayer wanted, but that is what VW head Toni Schmücker decided on Ascension Day in 1975; the rear engine was there to stay. Randolf Unruh writes in his history of the Type 2, an excellent reference (VW Bus/Transporter—Die Geschichte eines Welterfolgs, "The History of a Worldwide Success"), "Schmücker considered the Transporter to have no direct competition due to its particular design and mechanics."

While this attitude made sense in the middle of the decade when VW didn't have too many engines suitable for front installations, by the end of the decade, when VW did have engines designed for the front, spokespersons went through some verbal acrobatics defending a drive concept that was already outdated. They spoke of "consumer-oriented usefulness," "twelve different

Five all-wheel drive prototypes were built in 1978. The front-wheel drive was switchable. Transmission was via a four-speed manual transmission and torque converter.

The 1973 Bus had the new 1.8-liter engine with 69 DIN hp. Production hit a high that year, with 1200 units built per day. Photo shows a 1975 model.

The most important model changes and improvements VW Transporter T2:

1967: August, introduction of the new Transporter Type 2/T2. One-piece windshield without center strip, larger windows. Front ball joint axle without link pins. Semi-trailing link rear axle without auxiliary reduction gear on the wheels. Dual-circuit braking system, 55-liter fuel tank. New ventilation system, new heater controls, new dashboard. Cab doors with crank windows.

Bus: Quarter vent in the sliding door and in the left rear. Compressed air windshield washer, two-speed wipers. 1584 cm³ engine (47 DIN hp @ 4000 rpm), also supported at rear cross member. Special model with steel crank sunroof (previously folding sunroof). Models with wall separating cab from cargo area: spare tire under front seats; bus and Kombi, spare tire standing on left of engine.

1968: January, high-roof van with plastic roof (previously steel roof), sliding door extra.

August, new door handles with press buttons (as seen in Types 1 and 3), 540-watt generator. Symbols on indicator lights, wipers secured using cap nuts, improved noise insulation. Rear engine mount on double taper roller bearing, modified transmission housing. Standard hazard lights. Brake booster available at extra cost.

1969: August, engine modified (larger oil ducts, more powerful oil pump). Pre-heating of engine air controlled by thermostat, two oil pressure regulation valves. Collapsible steering column, reinforcements on front frame and axle mounting. Interior light controlled by door contact switch.

Bus: Make-up mirror in passenger sun visor, reinforced front doors.

Special editions: improved trim and bumper rails.

US models: Theft protection with ignition key warning.

1970: August, 50 DIN hp engine with stationary fan installed (double intake channels in cylinder head with forked intake pipes). New carburetor with recirculation channel, new material for crankcase, fan pulley enlarged by 5 mm, modified oil-bath air filter with thermostat. New steering knuckle with attached forged pitman arm, front disc brakes. Enlarged rear brakes with brake proportioning valve, optional power brakes. Reinforced drive shafts. 5 1/2 J x 14 wheels with flat Type 3 hubcaps. Sliding door lock with bowden cable.

1971: August, available 1.7-liter/66 DIN hp @ 4800 rpm. Flat engine from VW Type 4 (not in pickup), 1679 cm³ displacement, bore x stroke 90 x 66 mm. Engine mounts and transmission modified, 185 SR 14 tires (1.7-liter), reinforced body. Modified braking system. Brake servo (standard for the 1.7-liter). Auxiliary fan for heating. Rear bumper raised 20 mm, quarter vents in passenger compartment dropped. Air vents in cab doors, fuel filler moved to rear, new filler cap. Larger taillights, modified license plate illumination. Improved noise insulation.
September, three millionth Type 2 built.

1972: August, adaptations to meet stricter US emission standards, 1.7-liter engine with paper air filter. Longer intake pipes, engine mounts modified for installation of automatic transmission (only for 1.7-liter, 62 DIN hp with automatic). ZF cam-and-lever steering replaces previous cam-and-lever steering. Floor elements with deformation zones for improved passive safety, reinforced bumpers. Step ahead of front wheel arch (not visible with doors closed). 1.7-liter: Cover in rear panel, held in place by quick release fasteners. Warm air vents on top of dashboard on left and right. New interior colors. Control stalk on right under steering wheel, new wiper motor. Larger front turn signals installed near air intake. 14-mm brake pads, brake fluid reservoir under driver's seat.

1973: August, 1.8-liter double carburetor engine with 68 DIN hp (fuel injected version for US and Canada) replaces 1.7-liter. Modifications to 1.6-liter engine: new cylinder head alloy, reinforced exhaust valve stems, AC alternator. Fuel tank filler cover dropped for all models, standard seatbelts. Sliding door look with automatic latch, interior door knob from Types 1 and 4. Reinforced transmission housing. Final drive ratio 7/34 (manual transmission 1.8-liter).

Optional: Parking heater, headlight wipers.

November, delivery of Type 2 with 1.8-liter begins.

1974: Improved driver and passenger seats. 1.6-liter gets paper air filter. 1.8-liter engine with manual transmission can now pull higher weight (for trailers with brakes).

1975: July, four millionth Transporter built.

August, displacement increased from 1.8 to 2.0 liters (1970 cm³), 94-mm bore, 71- mm stroke, 70 DIN hp @ 4200 rpm. Radial tires, brake booster standard, different 4th gear and final drive ratios for 2.0-liter engine. 2.0-liter available with automatic transmission.

All models: standard brake regulation valve in rear, larger clutch, modified transmission ratios.

1976: August, full model line includes 8 base models and 17 special models. New VW radios.

Bus: Bulkhead behind front seats dropped, passenger seat now adjustable.

1.6-liter: Smaller intake valves, larger clutch disk for 2.0-liter.

1977: Four-and-a-half millionth VW Transporter.

August, improvements for bus. New steering wheel, new paint colors. L bus with two sliding windows instead of quarter vents in passenger area (extra cost for base bus and Kombi).

All models: Dual-circuit braking system with front discs and brake regulation valve.

1978: Eight-seater special edition: 2.0-liter engine, silver metallic paint, special equipment.
All models: Three-point automatic seatbelts for driver and passenger.

1979:	Prototype VW Bus Safari: Based on Camper, with addition of headlight grilles, driving lights, winch in front, wider fenders, sunroof. Side windows with curtains, tinted windows. Additional instruments, swivel passenger seat. Limited-slip differential, higher ground clearance, 205 R 14 tires. Price: Approx. DM 20,000. Not mass-produced.
	All-wheel drive VW bus prototype.
	July, production of T2 ends.

vehicle and engine combinations available to almost anybody" that people would examine and rate according to "cost, handling, roominess, size, comfort, safety, usefulness for different purposes, and image." The summation of this effort was to state that the old rear engine concept had been determined to be the best solution for installation in a vehicle class that could pull "one metric ton," although this included the fact that "a flat engine had to be installed under the floor." And even if it seems today that VW was trying to turn a liability into a virtue, it must be noted that while the third Transporter generation (EA 162—development order 162) was the end of the rear engine concept, it was in no way outdated.

The VW designers took front-end styling cues from the larger LT models; it didn't take much imagination to see the wider grill and integrated headlights from the square LT in the Transporter. The new body was 125 mm wider than the T2. According to VW, the decision to widen the body was made in consideration of certain export markets, such as the Scandinavian and Benelux countries

The third-generation T3 was offered as a Kombi, double-cab, pickup, van or bus. Many other model combinations were also available from the factory. The sales brochure listed a total of nine possibilities. The more powerful engine that was desperately needed was not among the list.

that wanted room for three people across. "With its 1.85 m, handling isn't quite as good as the old model," according to the magazine *Mot* in their first test of the new T3. They continued, "Parking is easier though, with a 2-m smaller turning circle balancing out the widened body." This was due in part to the new very precise rack-and-pinion steering, and to the new chassis. There were double wishbones in the front as well as struts and a stabilizer bar. In the rear was the well-known semi-trailing link suspension, albeit improved using mini-block coil springs, which in turn improved suspension reaction."

With corners and edges: This picture shows the three generations of the Transporter. The curb weight of the new van was 1385 kg. With the 1.6-liter engine, a top speed above 110 km/h was not possible. The more powerful engine went up to 127 km/h, albeit with difficulty.

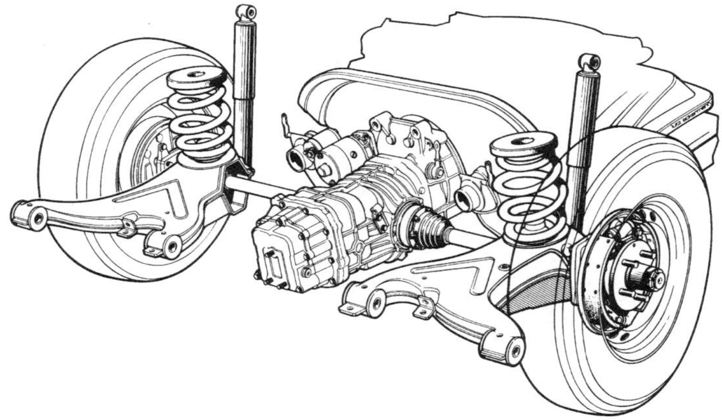

Above right:
Not much had changed on the semi-trailing link rear axle. On the other hand, the front axle saw a large number of modifications. Wheel location was controlled by double wishbones, progressive coil springs with inner telescopic shock absorbers, and a stabilizer bar.

That the bus was more stable on the road was also due to the track increase in the front from 1395 to 1570 mm and in the rear from 1455 to 1570 mm. "The new VW bus is neutral up to the limit," according to VW. They got support on this point from *Auto, Motor und Sport*: "The handling of the VW bus while cornering is helped not only by the modified axles but also by the wider track and improved axle load distribution with 51% on the front axle and 49% on the rear. This helped to reduce body roll and the tendency to oversteer. Handling has improved and is much closer to that of a passenger car." This praise could also be carried over to the interior design. The plain functional gray interior was gone. The dashboard and cab design reminded one more of the Golf and Passat. The improved instrument panel and dash was well thought out and ergonomic.

The brake system was from the previous model, with fixed-caliper disc brakes in the front and self-adjusting drums in the rear. The 2.0-liter models came with a power brake booster. The floor pan of the new Transporter was designed using computers, and resulted in a 100-mm lower entry height compared to its predecessor, and also did away with the cross members. This meant a low center of gravity and lower weight. The van with the 1.6-liter engine has a curbweight of 1365 kg. The GVWR of 2360 kg meant that almost one metric ton could be loaded into the vehicle. With the 2.0-liter power plant, the T3 weighed 30 kg more.

The rear engines were still air-cooled, four-cylinder, and carbureted. In addition to the 1.6-liter flat-four (37 kW/50 DIN hp with a maximum torque of 104 Nm at 2400 rpm) was the 2.0-liter from the previous model (51 kW/70 DIN hp and a maximum torque of 140 Nm at 3000 rpm). The larger engine cost DM 1125 extra; an automatic transmission cost an additional DM 1543.

Modern times: With the change from T2 to T3, body-in-white construction was now done using robots. Modern engines were installed in the Transporter starting in September 1982: two new water-cooled 1.9-liter flat-four engines replaced the old air-cooled engines—the water-cooled engines had arrived.

Both of the engines were used in the previous model. Modifications were made, though, for use in the T3. This included valve lifters (used by VW for the first time), electronic ignition, and digital idle stabilization (DIS). More drastic changes were made to the 1.6-liter engine. As for the 2.0 liter available since 1972, the cooling fan was now attached to the crankshaft. Air filter, alternator, distributor, and fuel pump were also relocated. This meant a much lower engine compartment and a cargo area lowered by 200 mm. "With this change, VW designers have managed to lower the floor to the level of a car with a classic drive design (front engine, rear drive)." (A pat on the back for VW by VW.) They were joined by *Auto, Motor und Sport* who applauded and congratulated VW on creating a "gigantic cargo area behind the rearmost bench." With the larger (by 75% according to VW) rear door and the larger sliding door on the side, it was also much more easily accessible. The sliding door design was similar to that used in the LT.

With a final drive ratio of 5.43, the 1.6-liter Transporter could go 110 km/h according to the factory. The 2.0-liter (compression 7.5:1) went 127 km/h (122 km/h with automatic transmission). The magazine *Mot* even got it up to 135 km/h. At that speed, though, fuel economy was as low as 14 mpg. "The true driving pleasure and relatively good fuel economy achieved during the test (18 mpg)

The new engines were much quieter with only slightly more output. This meant a job for well-known tuner Gerhard Oettinger whose Okrasa system gave many 1950s Beetles wings. Oettinger promised between 95 (T 1900V — carburetor) and 120 DIN hp (T 2300E — injection). Later Oettinger even installed a 3.2-liter Porsche engine in the rear of the Transporter.

Model: Type 2/T3 bus L 2.0
Built: 1979-82
Engine: 4-cylinder, flat-four
Valves: ohv, central camshaft
Displacement: 1913 cm^3
Bore x stroke: 94.0 x 71.0
DIN hp (kW) @ rpm:
70 (51) @ 4200
Drive: rear wheels
Carburetion:
two downdraft Solex PDSIT
Transmission: 4F, 1R
Brakes:
front discs, rear drums
Top speed: 127 km/h
Curb weight kg: 1440
Tires: 185 SR 14
Wheelbase: 2460 mm
Track f/r: 1570/1570 mm
L x W x H:
4570 x 1845 x 1950 mm

become most apparent on roads with many curves. No axle tramping or rolling with a loaded rear. This was something that its predecessor usually surprised you with during fast cornering. Good directional stability."

The most luxurious VW Bus (known as the Caravelle starting in 1983) was the Carat, recognizable from the outside by the alloy wheels and double headlights. These were also available as options in the "normal" Caravelle. This picture was taken in 1987.

The Water-cooled Engine and the Diesel Transporter

The era of air-cooled engines ended in the 1983 model year. In September 1982 VW introduced two new 1.9-liter water-cooled engines with 60 and 78 DIN hp. The base 1.9-liter engine had a single carburetor and an output of 44 kW/60 DIN hp @ 3700 rpm (max. torque 140 Nm @ 2200 rpm). The 57 kW (78 DIN hp) at 4400 rpm in the more powerful engine was due to a Pierburg downdraft two-stage carburetor, modified intake manifolds, and camshaft. Maximum torque here was 150 Nm @ 2600 rpm.

A good two years before, the 1.6-liter diesel engine from the Golf was installed in the Transporter. The engine output was 37 kW/50 DIN hp in the Golf but only 46 in the Transporter. To fit the engine in the Transporter, the inline four was tilted 50° to the left. Other engines were added over the years. In the 1985 model year, a 1.9-liter gasoline engine with 66 kW/90 DIN hp and digital fuel

In September 1985, Volkswagen presented the Multivan Westfalia edition. This combination of bus and camper got a lot of praise. VW therefore added this "economical family car" to the standard Transporter model line in 1986.

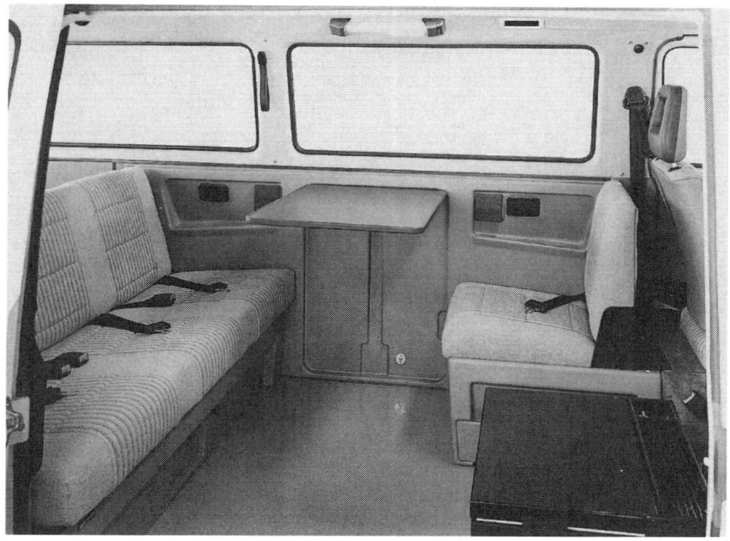

Model: Type 2/T3 Multivan TD
Built: 1980–91
Engine: 4-cylinder inline diesel, water-cooled
Valves: ohc
Displacement: 1588 cm³
Bore x stroke: 76.5 x 86.4 mm
DIN hp (kW) @ rpm: 70 (51) @ 4500
Drive: rear wheels
Fuel injection: Bosch fuel injection, KKK turbo
Transmission: 4F, 1R
Brakes: front discs, rear drums
Top speed: 127 km/h
Curb weight: 1480 kg
Tires: 185 R 14 C
Wheelbase: 2460 mm
Track f/r: 1585/1570 mm
L x W x H: 4570 x 1845 x 1960 mm

injection was added. It was already known then that a 2.1-liter with 112 DIN hp would be added in the following spring. At first, the 90 DIN hp engine was only available in the Caravelle Carat. Starting in the 1986 model year, it was available in all models (now all called the "Caravelle"). With computer-controlled fuel injection and catalytic converter, output rose to 68 kW/95 DIN hp @ 4500 rpm. Maximum torque was 154 Nm @ 2800 rpm. The 90 DIN hp gasoline engine disappeared with the introduction of the 2.1-liter. On the other hand, the Turbodiesel with Bosch injection and KKK turbo introduced at the same time remained in the price list until production of the T3 ended. The 1.9 TD output was 51 kW/70 DIN hp @ 4500 rpm. The flat torque curve meant maximum torque of 138 Nm at a low 2500 rpm. In 1986, the naturally aspirated diesel was

The "Magnum" special edition was based on the Multivan. It was introduced in the 1989 model year, a combination of the Multivan's equipment, including a refrigerator, with the looks of the Carat. Details from the Carat were also used in the Caravelle Coach, another special edition.

Model: Type 2/T3 double-cab Syncro Catalytic Converter
Built: 1985-90
Engine: 4-cylinder, flat-four, water-cooled
Valves: ohv, central camshaft
Displacement: 2109 cm³
Bore x stroke: 94.0 x 76.0 mm
DIN hp (kW) @ rpm: 95 (70) @ 4800
Drive: all-wheel drive
Fuel injection: Digifant
Transmission: 4F, 1off-road gear, 1R
Brakes: front discs, rear drums
Top speed: 141 km/h
Curb weight: 1595 kg
Tires: 185 R 14 C
(16": 195 R 16 PR 8**)**
Wheelbase: 2455 mm
(16": 2480 mm**)**
Track f/r: 1586/1554 mm
(16": 1597/1590 mm**)**
L x W x H: 4570 x 1845 x 1995 mm
(16": 4570 x 1890 x 2025 mm**)**

No other van manufacturer managed to completely harmonize engines, equipment and drive concepts. The "Tristar" was the luxury version of the double cab including all wheel-drive.

Left: In 1985, the Transporter Syncro with all-wheel drive was introduced. It was built by Steyr-Daimler-Puch. The all-wheel drive technology with a viscous clutch cost about DM 10,000 extra. The Syncro was also available with 16" wheels and reinforced body. This picture shows a 1989 Caravelle GL with 2.1-liter fuel-injected engine and 16" wheels.

enlarged to 1.7 liters and output increased to 42 kW/57 DIN HP @ 4500 rpm, with maximum torque of 103 Nm @ 2800 rpm. A three-speed automatic was available for the 57 kW engine and the fuel-injected engine. The all-wheel drive Syncro available starting in 1985 only came with the 2.1-liter engine with catalytic converter, with output of 70 kW @ 4800 rpm.

VW Camper (1950-90)

The history of the VW camper is really the history of the Westfalia camper. Of course there are many other firms that convert buses to campers, but without the Camping-Box from Westfalia, the VW camper California, Atlantic, and other models would never have been conceivable. The box originally appeared in 1951 as a special order for a British officer.

From the Camping Box to the Camper

That's all: After the front-wheel drive T4 was introduced, a limited number of T3 Syncros were built by Steyr in Graz in 1992.

This great wagon for the traveler was to represent the birth of the German motor camper. It was designed and built by Westfalia, located in Rheda-Wiedenbrück in the German State of North Rhine-Westfalia. The company was founded in 1844 by Johann Bernhard Knöbel, a blacksmith, who created his first carriage in 1876. His son, Franz, registered the name "Westfalia" in 1922, while Franz's son

The most important model changes and improvements VW Transporter T3:

1979: May, presentation of the T3 (EA 162—EA is Entwicklungsauftrag or development order). Completely redesigned.

June, start of production. Two engines: 1.6-liter (37 kW/50 DIN hp @ 3800 rpm, max. torque 103 Nm @ 2400 rpm), 2.0-liter (51 kW/70 DIN hp @ 4200 rpm, max. torque 137 Nm @ 3000 rpm). Completely new design, similar to the LT, larger windows. Available as van, Kombi, pickup and double-cab. Also seven-, eight-, and nine-seater bus.

1980: March, improved oil cooler for 1.6-liter.

May, redesigned cylinder head, modified exhaust mounting (1.6-liter).

August, 2.0-liter available with "mountain transmission." All models now have 17 digit VIN. Modification to voltage regulator.

September, VW Transporter with diesel engine from Golf introduced. 1.6-liter, 37 kW (50 DIN hp) @ 4200 rpm, max. torque 103 Nm @ 2000 rpm, top speed of 110 km/h, fuel economy: 22-26 mpg. Curb weight: 1510 kg, around 100 kg more than model with gasoline engine. GVWR: 2400 kg. Additional grill in the front. "D" on rear.

1981: January, black plastic cover on engine air intake openings. Increased towing weight. New radios.

February, diesel bus available for delivery.

April, 1.6-liter: modified ignition timing.

September, introduction of seven-seater special Caravelle edition. Two-tone paint. Chrome fenders with rubber trim. Rear window wiper/washer system. Frame head-rests for driver and passenger. Foldable armrests for all seats, improved seat padding and upholstery. Velour carpet, padded headliner. Dashboard available in brown or black. Added storage compartments. Three-point seatbelts in front, pre-wired for radio, protective grill for heated rear window, quarter vents in front, steel belted 185 SR 14 radials.

1982: September, new, water-cooled 1.9-liter flat-four engines with 60 and 78 DIN hp replaced previous air-cooled power plants (continued to be built for export to Argentina, Brazil, Mexico and South Africa). Alloy crankcase and cylinder head, crank-shaft supported in three main bearings, central camshaft. Engine weighs 95 kg. Wet cylinder running sleeves, bore x stroke 94 mm x 68.9 mm. Top speeds of 118 km/h and 130 km/h. Available 5-speed transmission. 78 DIN hp engine also available with three-speed automatic. Modified interior. Improved heating and ventilation, available with heat exchanger under rear bench (standard with automatic transmission). All models: power brake booster, hydraulic clutch and 185 SR 14 tires. Engine supported in three mountings (previously four), and shorter, moved 40 mm toward the rear. This put the drive shafts at exact right angles to the rear wheels (less wear). Additional cooler grill as in the diesel. GWVR: 2390 kg.

Caravelle special edition "Tone in Tune": special Pewter Gray paint, velour seat covers in black and silver. Gray velour carpeting. Frame headrests for all seats, safety belts.

Sliding windows on the side, tinted glass. Heat exchanger in passenger compartment. Rear fog lights. Engine: 1.9-liter/78 DIN hp.Total of 5.5 million Type 2s built.

1983: September, new marketing strategy. Transporter and Kombi now known as Transporter, bus is the Caravelle. Available as C, CL or GL.

Introduction of special edition bus "Caravelle Carat": 1.9-liter/90 DIN hp fuel-injected engine, 5-speed, power steering, and tachometer. Alloy wheels, side body trim, and rectangular double headlights. Swivel seats in the center, armrests, velour covers, carpeting, and radio/cassette.

1984: September, 1.9-liter: Corrosion protection for Transporter improved immensely. A rear bench that could be converted into a bed was available (bed padding stored in trunk). Cab available with sunroof.

Standard for all models: front headrests, reverse lights, and lockable fuel tank flap. Rear wiper with interval switch.

1985: February, transporter "Syncro" with permanent all-wheel drive via viscous clutch, developed by Steyr-Daimler-Puch in Austria, built in Graz. Body and engines from Germany. At first only available with 78 DIN hp carbureted engine.

August, introduction of 1.6-liter/70 DIN hp turbodiesel engine. 2.1-liter fuel-injected engine with 112 DIN hp. Also available with computer-controlled fuel injection and catalytic converter (output reduced to 95 DIN hp).

All models: Central fuse, relay and terminal box and one-key system. 1.9-liter with 90 DIN hp dropped, modifications to 1.9-liter/78 DIN hp (max. torque now 153 Nm, previously 141 Nm).

September, at the IAA in Frankfurt, VW introduced the "Multivan" camper study (Westfalia conversion).

1986: January, the six millionth Transporter is built.

New options: power windows and outside mirrors, cruise control and central door locking.

All models: asbestos-free clutch and brake pads.

September, Syncro now available with turbodiesel, 112 DIN hp and 95 DIN hp engines. For off-road use also available in 16" version (added special shocks, reinforced final drive, differential locks, stronger braking system). Reinforcements added to the body, plastic trim for enlarged wheel cutouts, off-road package, spare tire on left side of trunk.

"Multivan" available: Westfalia edition (later VW), including folding table, seats convertible into beds, bench seats with storage compartments, refrigerator, cupholders.

1987: New option of anti-lock braking system (ABS). Naturally aspirated diesel: now 1.7-liter (bore increased from 76.5 to 79.5 mm), output: 57 DIN hp, previously 50 DIN hp. Improved heating and ventilation, side outlets. Forced ventilation of rear passenger compartment, window antenna instead of whip.

	October, "Caravelle Coach" special edition: power steering, wide tires (205/70), lowered 30 mm, driver and passenger armrests, double headlights, carpeting, day/night rearview mirror, heat exchanger in passenger compartment, rear window defroster and heated wipers, full wheel covers, among other extras. Seven- or eight-seater, three engines (70/95/112 DIN hp).
1988:	September, "Tristar" special edition, double-cab based on Syncro, with double grill, carpeting, cloth seats with armrests, running boards, bumpers with overriders, glass roof, wheel covers, roll bar, foglights.
	"Multivan Magnum" special edition: Exterior from Carat (including double headlights, bumpers and side trim). Interior included VW's seat/bed system, power steering, interval wipers and rear wipers, sliding window in sliding door, frame headrests in passenger compartment, cigarette lighter.
1989:	March, 25,000th Transporter Syncro built in Graz.
	September, engine and transmission modifications. 2.1-liter/112 DIN hp dropped. Fuel- injected engine with regulated catalytic converter, output reduced to 92 DIN hp; to 95 DIN hp for Syncro and automatic.
	All models: double rectangular headlights (Multivan/Caravelle), storage compartment in driver's door, day/night rearview mirror, trip odometer and clock, cigarette lighter, interval wipers, lockable glove compartment. Only Multivan/Caravelle: rear window defroster, 65A alternator, tinted windows, 205/70 tires (Caravelle GL). Price of Syncro models reduced by DM 2,900.
1990:	March, 40th anniversary of VW Transporter on March 8.
	May, introduction of the new T4 Transporter.
	August, delivery of T4 begins; Syncro continued to be built by Steyr-Daimler-Puch.
1992:	March, "Limited Last Edition": Multivan with 4 x 2 drive. Aluminum 6J x 14 wheels, body-colored bumpers (Orly blue metallic). Body lowered by 30 mm, power steering. Heated outside mirrors, tachometer. Stereo/cassette, four speakers. Limited edition of 2500. Prices: DM 38,750 (Turbo-D), DM 39,150 (68 kW/92 DIN hp gasoline). Optional: Tornado Red paint (price reduced by DM 480).
	September, production of T3 Syncro Transporter built by Steyr ends.

(also named Franz) got a patent for the trailer hitch ball in 1931; even today, there is no better way to connect a vehicle with a trailer.

Of course, the company in Wiedenbrück soon found a use for the new invention. The first Westfalia travel trailer was introduced in 1935. This was the "Landstreicher" (the "Tramp"), which could sleep four adults, had a cooking area and a lot of storage room. After WWII, the company began to specialize in building trailers for passenger cars. In 1949, Westfalia introduced a travel trailer for VW (400 kg), as well as a special VW trailer that could carry 250 kg (this cost DM 765). In 1951, the Camping Box was introduced, which

Since the 1950s, the Type 2 has defended its position as the most popular camping and vacation vehicle for Germans. The first camping setup was Westfalia's camping box introduced in 1951. An awning and other accessories were introduced in 1952. Shown is a 1960 bus with 1961 camping equipment.

could be installed transversely directly behind the front bench. The setup was installed in the van and taken out again Sunday night. From Monday to Saturday, the vehicle was a regular van.

If the two drawers in the box weren't enough, a cabinet was available. The wood furniture had rolling doors and exactly fitted the cargo area above the engine. Height was more of a problem. Clothes could not be hung but had to be laid flat. What is a camper without sleeping arrangements? The Westfalia box provided for this as well (and according to the ads could also be used as furniture for your home). At least three people could sleep in the vehicle, as long as they were shorter than 6 ft; this is something that is still true for California models today. Just a reminder: the width of a VW was not more than 157 cm, so more than three in a bed would not have been that comfortable.

In addition, two children could sleep in the cab, as long as the seatback was raised into place. Even a separate wash area was available that could be installed on the rear of the two side doors. Cooking was also possible, of course, using the one burner stove (run on gasoline or spirits), a standard part of the package. According to the price list (the first one appeared in March 1953), the box ("with 4 high-quality cushions") cost DM 595, the wash compart-

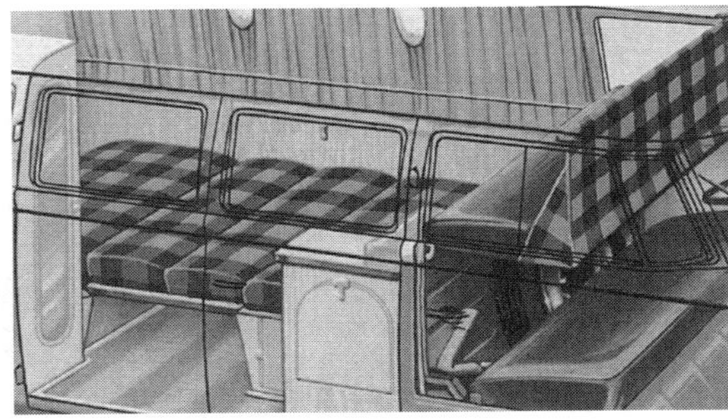

ment above the engine cost DM 125, and the "wash and shaving cabinet" that could be installed on the rear side door cost DM 62.50.

Although the success of the box wasn't all too great in Germany, an awning designed to fit the bus was introduced in 1952. The awning had stripes and was almost as long as the bus. A year later a hinged roof flap was available. Most of the camping boxes were sold in the US; Westfalia published its first color brochure designed to make the US drivers' mouths water for the camping addition to the VW. In the mid-1950s cooperation between Wolfsburg and Wiedenbrück increased. Under contract from the van department, Westfalia converted used vans. In 1958, Westfalia opened a camper assembly line. A year before that, the SO-23 camping box is mentioned; the official VW Camper was available in 1958 as a 1959 model. In 1960, the Transporter debuted as a true camper: a special interior, insulation, and a 90-liter water tank were part of the standard package, which also included storage closets and curtains.

"Take a car trip in your own hotel—no more unfulfilled dreams. This is a luxury everyone can afford," according to the VW ads, which extolled the virtues of the Camper ("VW Camping de Luxe"),

In 1961, the Westfalia Camper was officially added to the VW model line. The brochure showed exactly how to convert the van into a sleeping area, with room in the cab for children to sleep.

Right:
Success: The Joker and Club Joker models put Westfalia at the top in terms of equipment, workmanship, and also price. The Joker 1 package, without base vehicle, cost more than DM 11,500. Lower caption in ad: Car for everyday use, Vehicle for business and hobbies, Camper for vacation and freetime.

1973 Westfalia Camper with pop top, fresh-water tank, installed cabinets and other typical camper accessories. The 100,000th Camper had been built two years earlier, in 1971.

Westfalia Die Multimobile

WESTFALIA

Präzision auf Rädern

Auto für alle Tage.
Fahrzeug für Geschäft und Hobby.
Wohnmobil für Ferien und Freizeit.

In the fall of 1988, VW presented their own camper, the "California." It was based on the successful Joker model and was also built by Westfalia, but cost DM 10,000 less.

The California was introduced together with the luxurious "Atlantic," which was also available with high roof or pop top. Both models were sold through the VW dealer network and came with the full factory warranty.

With the T3, the yacht builder Dehler in Meschede got into the camper business. Their "Profi" (which was also available in a "Junior" model with pop top) was designed as a combination elegant camper and mobile office.

Model: Type 2/T3 Atlantic
Built: 1988-90
Engine: 4-cylinder, flat-four, water-cooled
Valves: ohv
Displacement: 2109 cm^3
Bore x stroke: 94 x 76 mm
DIN hp (kW) @ rpm: 92 (68) @ 3700
Drive: rear wheels
Fuel injection: Digi-Jet, catalytic converter
Transmission: 5F, 1R
Brakes: front discs, rear drums
Top speed: 133 km/h
Curb weight: 1800 kg
Tires: 185/70 R 14 C
Wheelbase: 2460 mm
Track f/r: 1585/1570 mm
L x W x H: 4605 x 1845 x 2080 mm (2610 with high roof)

adding it to the official Transporter program in 1961. This was definitely the end of the camping box era (even if it was still available for purchase).

The camper business didn't really get going until the second generation Transporter was introduced for the 1968 model year. Business was especially big in the US. On March 8, Westfalia celebrated the 30,000th camper that came off the assembly line (75% were exported). Business kept increasing at an amazing pace. In 1969, 80 Campers (and 5 "Fridolin" Type 147) came off the assembly line each day. Another record was broken in 1971 when the 100,000th Camper left the assembly line in Wiedenbrück. Westfalia was building 125 Campers a day. Around 19,000 of the 22,417 units were bound for the US. That things didn't keep going up and up was due to the oil crisis in 1973. Sales in the most important US market dropped by a horrifying 35%. By the middle of the decade, though, the situation had gotten a bit better. Westfalia used the Helsinki and Berlin models to bridge the gap until the third - generation Transporter and the Joker were introduced. The Camper "represents the current level of mobile camping technology," according to the specialty magazine *Promobil* in a chronicle of the Westfalia published in 1994. The Joker set new standards in terms of quality and workmanship and had a well-thought-out equipment list, even if the price was high. The Joker package added DM 8440 to the price, almost as much a brand new Mexican-built Beetle. Of course, the price of the Transporter had to be added to this, which meant another DM 18,000. At the dealers, the Campers were dealt with as "two-invoice vehicles." One invoice was from VW for the base vehicle, while the other was from the camper manufacturer. Accounting didn't get any easier until 1988 when VW added a slimmed-down US version of the Joker (the "California") to the US model list. The somewhat better -equipped "Atlantic" followed a year after that.

Camper Conversion Companies

The Weinsberg body factory built a camper very similar to the Joker. This was the Terra Camper. Weinsberg, founded in 1912, built their first camper, the Cosmos, in 1969 using a Fiat 238 as the base. VW's own campers appeared in 1977 based on the LT model line. The Terra campers, with high or pop top, appeared in 1979 with the third Transporter generation. One of the special things about this vehicle was the gas-fired heating unit with warm-air circulation.

Even the yacht manufacturer, Dehler, got into the camper ring with the third Transporter generation. The "Profi" was possibly the most elegant way to drive a VW Transporter. A variable interior was designed to be used as both mobile office and camper. The DM

25,000 for this edition got you a TV, a shower, and many other special accessories.

Many other companies also offered Transporter conversions, but Carthago campers were popular. Carthago was founded in 1979, and first specialized in building conversion kits for people to buy and install themselves. In 1986 they concentrated more on the VW Transporter and even offered complete vehicles, sold under the "Malibu" label. This included five different base models with high roof or pop top. At the end of the 1980s, up to 900 complete vehicles left the assembly line in their factory near Ravensburg on Lake Constance.

Seen at every campground: Campers based on the Transporter. On the right is a VW T3 Atlantic. On the left the T2 Camper from a small Swabian company Gray, the "Grawomobil."

Reminds one of a Westfalia Joker, the Weinsberg Terra.

The road to the Camper

1951: April, Westfalia camping box introduced.

1952: Optional: roof light added extra height for standing.

1954: Optional: bar with ten cocktail glasses, chemical toilet.

1958: Westfalia added to the official VW model line, approx. 1000 are sold (since 1952). Box with installed gas stove and larger wardrobe installed above engine compartment (some clothes could be hung). Sidewall trim, some insulation. Camper production on Westfalia assembly line.

1960: VW Kombi with SO23 camping setup available: camper with installed additions.

1962: Westfalia camper special edition 34: camping setup with plastic top (gray and white, previously wood grain finish). Hinged roof flap.

1963: Special edition 35: same as 34, but covered with wood trim.

Optional: Westfalia camping setup with polyester folding roof (DM 1675) raised on driver's side, interior height, 2.47 m (8 ft). Sleeping room for two (hammocks).

1966: Westfalia camper special edition 42: Interior trim, roof storage area, refrigerator with water tank, hand pump and foldable table. Clothing closet with mirror to be used as washing up area, corner cabinet on left; storage compartments in front and rear with padding, rear bed. Price for the Westfalia addition with pop top on September 1, 1965: DM 1850.

1967: Optional: Elektrolux refrigerator for 12V or 220V (DM 410)–only available for SO 44. Two roofs available–polyester folding roof and popup roof.

1968: Camper special edition 60 based on the new Type 2/T2. Popup roof, folding roof, and sunroof available.

. March, 30,000th Westfalia camper built.

1969: May, 50,000th Westfalia camper built.

Production of Weinsberg camper begins (based on Fiat 238).

1971: 100,000th Westfalia camper built.

1976: Camper special edition 73 Westfalia Helsinki/Berlin: Plastic top (wood grain), checkered seat fabric. Three to five beds depending on equipment, gas cooker, Nirosta sink, 28-liter fresh water tank and 50-liter insulating compartment (available as freezer chest); high roof or pop top. Spare tire box available on front of vehicle.

Also available: two conversion kits. You only had to make sure to order the vehicle with the needed mountings and roof reinforcements. 175,000th camper built.

1979: Westfalia Joker model introduced: Pop top with luggage rack above cab. Swivel front seats, kitchen area with cabinets on left, foldable seat bench in rear, double-glazed windows all around, fresh water tank, gas cooker with tank, refrigerator, second battery, gas-fired heater. Models: Joker 2, Club Joker, Joker 7 (base model). Joker addition, DM 8685.

September, at IAA, VW presents two studies: the "Weekender" (with high roof, rectangular headlights one above the other) and the "Traveller Jet" (glass roof top, rectangular headlights side by side).

Weinsberg body factory: Terra Camper with high roof or pop top.

Carthago founded.

1981: September, Westfalia Joker: Furniture in beige instead of oak, new seat covers, color of dashboard and steering wheel matched.

1982: Presentation of Dehler Profi: Plastic high roof in sandwich style, TV, shower. Refrigerator, gas stove, sink and toilet. Variable interior, seats for six. Could be used as a mobile office or camper; additional cost starting at DM 24,000.

1984: September, 250,000th Westfalia Camper.

1985: VW Multivan (Westfalia conversion).

1986: Carthago Malibu camper available.

1988: October, Volkswagen presents their first VW Camper, the "California," at the Camper show in Essen. It has a Westfalia conversion, based on the Joker, and could be ordered with high roof or pop top. Front grill with double headlights. Plastic bumper cover, front skirt, swivel driver and passenger seats with armrests, power steering, tachometer and clock, rear window defroster, rear wiper, tinted windows on side, wheel covers. Interior: insulation in all body hollows, side and roof trim, curtains all around, 55-liter fresh water tank, 20-liter waste tank, 8 kg gas tank, two-burner stove, 42-liter refrigerator, foldable rear bench with bed padding above engine compartment, foldable table, double bed in roof. Stickers and insignia. Engines: 51 kW/70 DIN hp Turbo diesel with 5-speed, 57 kW/78 DIN hp gasoline with 5-speed or automatic; 68 kW/92 DIN hp fuel injection with regulated catalytic converter and five-speed; and 70 kW/95 DIN hp with fuel injection, regulated catalytic converter and automatic transmission. Prices starting at DM 45,263 (Turbo D with pop top).

1989: September, "Atlantic" Camper. Like "California" but with complete side trim, power mirrors painted in body color, dash in light gray, different seat covers, second battery, charger, parking heater with timer, cupholders etc. Engines: 51 kW/70 DIN hp Turbo diesel with 5-speed; 68 kW/92 DIN hp fuel injection and computer-controlled catalytic converter and five-speed; and 70 kW/95 DIN hp with fuel injection, computer-controlled catalytic converter and automatic transmission. Prices starting at DM 52,109.40 (Turbo D with pop top).

das AUTO MOTOR UND SPORT
IN FRANKFURT GESEHEN UND GEFAHREN
Großer Testbericht:
das AUTO MOTOR UND SPORT beurteilt den VW 1500
S-MT 646
E 1418 D
WER GARANTIERT DIE GARANTIE?
FRISCHER TABAK FÜR PFEIFENRAUCHER
PARKEN MIT SANFTER GEWALT
HEFT 21
7. OKTOBER 1961
DM 1.50
Schweiz Fr. 1.70, Österreich S. 11.–, Schweden SKr. 2.10 inkl. oms., Dänemark dKr. 3.25, Niederlande HfL. 1.50

Chapter 6

VW Type 3 1500/1600 (1961-73)

Left:
Type 3: A new model from Volkswagen caused a sensation. This meant comprehensive press coverage. The first comprehensive test of the third independent design from VW (after the Beetle and Transporter) was published in October 1961.

Model: VW 1500 Limousine
Built: 1961-63
Engine: 4 cylinder, boxer
Valves:
ohv, central camshaft
Displacement: 1493 cm^3
Bore x stroke: 83 x 69 mm
DIN hp (kW) @ rpm:
45 (33) @ 3800
Drive: rear wheels
Carburetion:
1 Solex 32 PHN-1
Transmission: 4F, 1R
Brakes: drums f+r
Top speed: 130 km/h
Curb weight: 880 kg
Tires: 6.00-15
Wheelbase: 2400 mm
Track f/r: 1310/1346 mm
L x W x H:
4225 x 1605 x 1475 mm

Everyone knew what the VW 1500/Type 3 looked like long before it was available for purchase. It was fairly obvious that Wolfsburg was planning a new, larger model (which VW considered "icing on the cake"), especially as the head of VW, Heinrich Nordhoff, had hinted at just such a model at the 1960 Geneva Car Salon. The first details about the car were publicized through the head of exports at the factory, Manuel Hinke, and through the US press agency, UPI, at the end of March. A few hours later, Nordhoff denied there was such a model, but eventually gave in and confirmed "the wink from Hinke" (*Der Spiegel* issue 15/1960) that they were planning a larger model. The first photos of the car were available a year later, a good six months before the official introduction at the Frankfurt IAA in September 1961. *Auto, Motor und Sport* published a comprehensive test of a preproduction model in May. The most important realization was that the VW 1500 was not a Beetle, but it was a true Volkswagen.

The Design

In terms of its main components, body, chassis and engine, the VW Type 3 was a completely new design, but was based on the well-known Beetle concept.

The Body

Basically the new Volkswagen was an all-enveloping body that consisted of three metal sections: the front and rear of the car were the two smaller sections and the larger third section was the passenger compartment. Like its older brother, the Beetle, the body was open on the bottom and then bolted to the floor pan. The body, only available as a two-door, consisted of front and rear sections: the front cross member, the inner quarter panels, the roof, lower side-members, and the front and rear cover panels. The dashboard was

welded in and was used as a supporting member. The outer skin and front fenders (bolted on) were made of 0.8-mm sheet steel; doors, hood and trunk, and rear fenders were made of 0.75-mm sheet steel. The doors were 1068 mm wide and contained quarter windows and crank windows. The rear windows were popout windows. Laminated glass was extra.

Below:
Flat: The fan was behind the engine directly on the crankshaft in the VW 1500. This was different in the Type 1. In addition, the fan belt that drove the generator was covered.

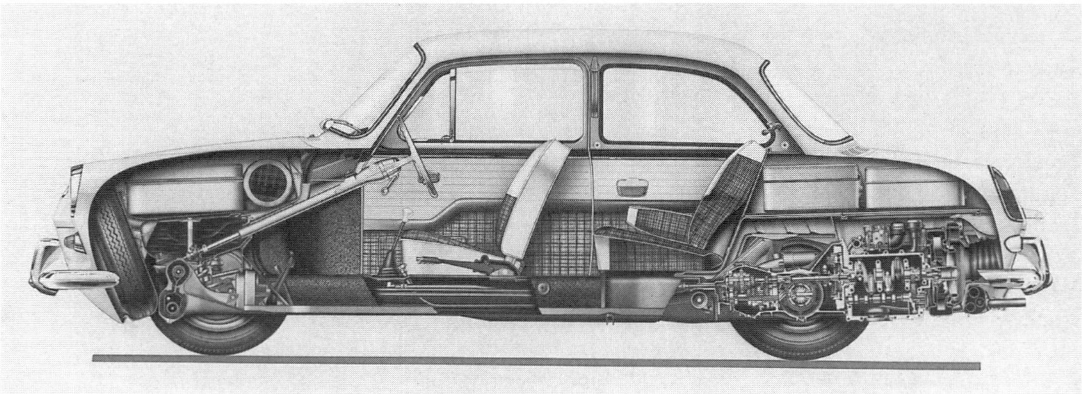

Left:
Sensible lines: The VW 1500, introduced at the Frankfurt IAA in September 1961.

Many changes compared to the Beetle were also to be seen on the front axle. The lower torsion bars ran the width of the vehicle and crossed in the center. The stabilizer was located in the upper transverse member. In addition, supporting ball joints were used instead of link pins and king pins.

The Chassis

If you knew Volkswagens, you already knew what the chassis in this mid-size VW would look like. The tubular backbone frame was well known and had been for 25 years. The same applied to the front axle design with trailing links and torsion bars. Compared to the Type 1 Beetle, the torsion bars were twice as long. They no longer ended at the center of the axle but ran from one side of the vehicle to the other and were jointed. This gave the VW 1500 a noticeably softer suspension. The ends of the axles were supported by rubber bushings. The rear swing-arm axle was also typical VW. It was now possible, however, to remove the rear axle together with the engine/transmission unit all at once. This was made possible by the use of a subframe. Rubber dampers between the vehicle and the subframe meant the body was better isolated from road noise and engine vibration. VW engineers made great improvements over the Beetle by using cam-and-roller steering with steering dampers instead of the often-criticized and outdated worm-and-nut steering. The Type 3 rode on large 15" wheels like the Beetle. Only the VW 1500, though, enjoyed the new tire size 6.00 x 15 as well as duplex brakes in the front. This meant each shoe had its own brake cylinder.

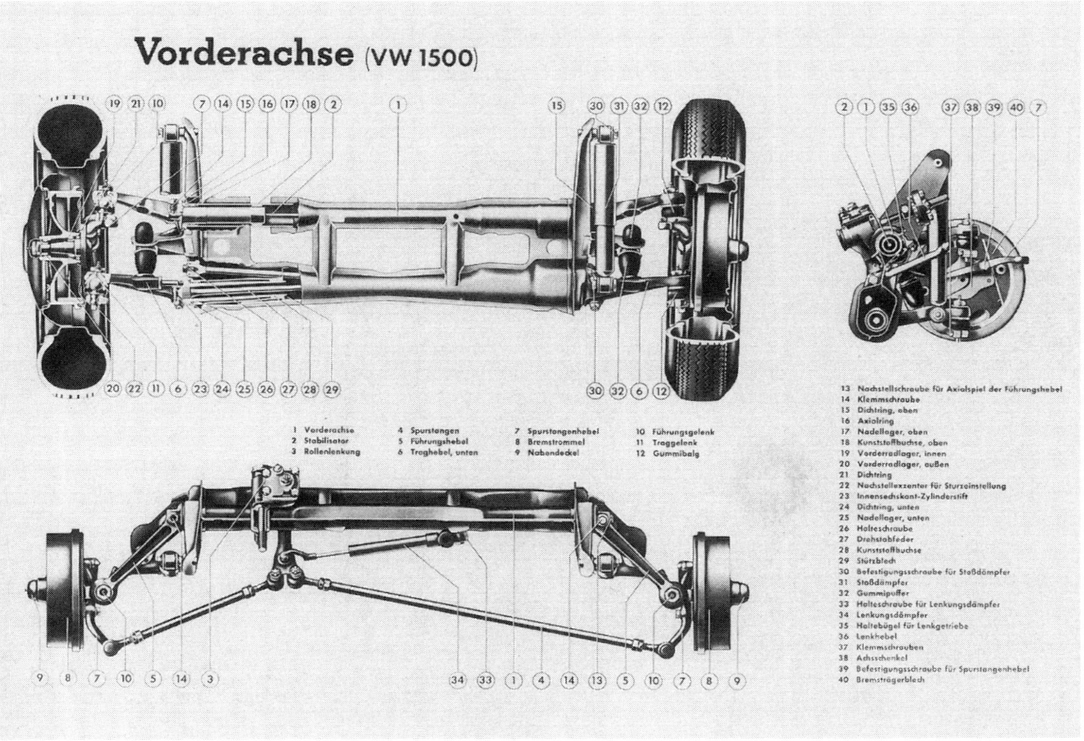

The floor pan of the Type 3. As in the Beetle, this was a tubular backbone frame with a 2400-mm wheelbase. Front and rear track were almost identical between the two vehicles.

The Engine

As in the Type 1, the Type 3 engine was an air-cooled four-cylinder boxer. Displacement was 1493 cm^3 (bore x stroke: 83 mm x 69 mm). The engine output was a moderate 45 DIN hp at 3800 rpm, a typically restricted engine designed to last a long time. As was typical of VW engines, the valves were actuated via push rods and rocker arms via a single camshaft installed on the side of the engine. VW had good reasons for using what was basically hand-me-down technology; they had to defend the reputation of the Beetle and the factory in terms of reliability and longevity.

The flat engine: It was basically the power plant used in the Type 1, except for the relocated fan.

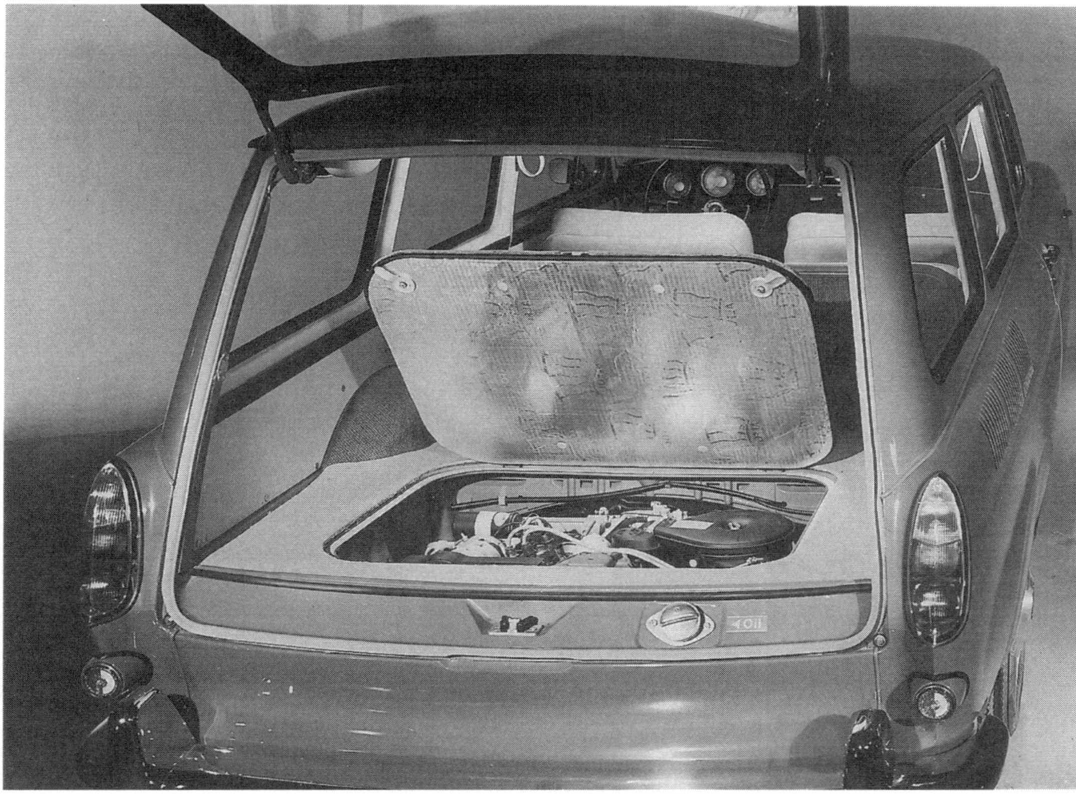

The rear engine meant that the trunk floor was high. Without the flat engine design, this model would never have been possible, "The advantages of the flat engine are more obvious in the wagon than in the sedan," a test report of the time stated.

To save design height, components such as fan, oil cooler, carburetor and generator were rearranged.

The crankcase was from the 1200 engine from 1960, except with a new crankshaft. The Type 3 engine also used a horizontal draft carburetor (Solex 32 PHN-I) instead of the downdraft carburetor used in the Beetle. The fan was relocated and attached directly to the crankshaft instead of the crankcase. Although the fan in the Type 3 had a smaller diameter, the amount of air supplied to the engine increased. Even better, the engine was now only 400 mm high. Airflow was slightly different than in the VW 1200 due to the relocation of the fan. The lower engine height also meant a somewhat larger luggage area in the rear. Access to the engine was through a removable floor plate in the rear trunk area, something found not only in Type 3 but also the Type 4 (introduced in 1968) and the third Transporter generation.

VW 1500 (1961-66)

"Any criticism of the shape of the VW 1500 will become pointless in time. People won't be talking about the shape but the car" (*Auto, Motor und Sport*, 1961)

Porsche engineers also had their hands on the VW 1500. The fine-tuning took place at the Porsche factory in Stuttgart-Zuffenhausen. The prototypes for VW had been built by the Stuttgart body specialist Reutter (later the Porsche body factory). In many ways, the VW 1500 seemed more grown up than the Beetle, except in one respect. There was no more room in the rear than in the Type 1, as they both had the same wheelbase. This meant though that the VW shops could easily use the new test stands that had been designed for the Beetle, without any major changes.

During the mid-1950s, VW had started a great effort to install test stands in the VW shops that allowed the mechanic to perform a thorough check of the vehicle in 12 to 15 minutes. The entire apparatus could be installed in a space smaller than 50 m^2 and was also suitable for smaller shops. The new vehicle only required a few additional tools that together cost a reasonable DM 1200.

Even at 4225 mm (160 mm longer than the Beetle), the VW 1500 was significantly shorter than the competition. The Opel Rekord was 29 cm longer, 14 cm due to the wheelbase alone. The wheelbase in the Ford was 17 cm longer with a total length that was 23 cm longer. Ford and Opel set the standards for mid-size cars. The biggest advantage of the Type 3 over the Beetle was that the Type

The car with two trunks: the luggage area in the front shared the space with a 40-liter fuel tank...

...while the rear trunk space was restricted by the engine compartment. Oil was added to the engine though the oil filler nozzle located just above the license plate. The dipstick was integrated in the cap.

3 had two larger luggage areas. In addition, driver and passenger had a bit more elbow room. The floor pan wasn't any wider, but because the Type 3 didn't get any narrower toward the front, as the Beetle did, it meant a little more room.

When compared to the standards of 1961 (and of the Beetle too), Wolfsburg's new mid-size car model cut a good figure, even if the outer shape wasn't all that exciting. They had built a faultless car, but it was a car that "wasn't going to upset anybody or get anybody excited" (*Auto, Motor und Sport*). The interior was in the simple VW style: three round instruments in the instrument panel with the speedometer (indicating up to 150 km/h) in the center. On

The speedometer sat front center. On the right was a clock, on the left the fuel gauge. The sliding levers in the center controlled the heating. The buttons on the far left, which can barely be seen in the picture, controlled the wipers and the lights.

the right was a clock, and on the left a fuel gauge as well as indicator lights for turn signals, parking lights, high beams, generator, and oil pressure. On the left was the switch panel, four ivory-colored knobs with chrome trim that reminded one a little of an old radio. These controlled windshield wipers and washer, parking lights, and headlights: two thumb wheels, one on top of the other, provided continuously variable control of the wiper speed and instrument panel lighting. The upper part of the dashboard was padded. Due to the typical Volkswagen rear engine concept, there wasn't a lot of room in the vehicle. Two people had enough room to bring along their luggage, but four people had to be very careful about how much luggage they packed. This was not only due to the narrow rear seat: the front trunk held 6.4 cu.ft., while the rear held 7.0 cu.ft.

The four-seater Cabriolet, built by Karmann, was introduced at the IAA in 1961.

**Type 3 convertible.
The brochures were already printed; the price was set at DM 8200. But testing showed the body didn't have enough torsional stiffness and so it was never added to the model line.**

With a full 40-liter tank, the 1500 weighed 873 kg., and 377 kg. could be loaded into the car. The first tests showed that the new VW handled well. The tendency of the car to oversteer due to the design was significantly lower than in the Beetle. Performance and top speed (around 130 km/h) were also nothing to be ashamed of. Something that wasn't really obvious in the first test, but would be criticized more and more, was the sensitivity to cross-winds, the brakes (people complained about the grabbing and the high pressures needed to push the pedal) and the clutch (VW enlarged the clutch diameter for the 1963 model year). What couldn't be changed was the inadequate ventilation, particularly when driving slowly. The heating actuation via rotary knob was also criticized severely until it was finally changed for the 1964 model year. VW ads for that new year indicated 28 improvements, which were calculated over a year (August 1, 1962 to August 1, 1963), but this actually included two model years.

With the introduction of the special edition, which cost as much as the previous standard model with 45 DIN hp (DM 6400), the base 1500 (now with the addition of "N" to the name) cost less than DM 6000. When the VW 1500S was replaced by the VW 1600TL, the name of the base car changed again, to 1500A. This model remained in the model line until July 1966 when it was replaced by the VW 1600, available with 45 DIN hp (A model) or 54 DIN hp (L model) and an engine with dual carburetors.

The Wagon

Opel was the leader in the station wagon market. Since 1953, 462,326 wagons had been registered in Germany, with more than 44% coming from Opel's Rüsselheim factory. VW introduced their wagon to try to gain a share of the market. Many people felt that the

On the assembly line: The 10,000th Type 3 was built in mid-December 1961, just three months after production had started. By the time production of the model ended, almost 2.5 million had been built.

wagon was the better choice of the "large" VW. The wagon was identical to the sedan up to the B pillar. Besides the obvious differences in roof, window area and sides, the major differences between the wagon and the sedan were in interior equipment: the fold-down armrest in the rear was dropped, slits for engine intake, ventilation and heating air were in the rear fenders. Air flowed to the intake manifold and fan through a channel welded to the quarter panel. The rear seat could be folded down, which meant a large flat cargo area. The cargo area was covered with a rubber mat. The hatch opened very wide.

The wagon was built starting in February 1962 and was offered in two versions; one could carry 375 kg and the other 460 kg. The chassis was identical in both (and was basically the same as in the sedan), but the stronger of the two had an additional torsion bar in the rear. The wagon was also available as an "S" version, as was the sedan starting in the 1964 model year.

VW 1500S

For the 1964 model year, Volkswagen increased its offering with the "S" models. "What VW drivers have been dreaming of in the VW 1200 for ten years, has become a reality for the VW 1500 after only two years. There's now a sporty version." This is how *Auto, Motor und Sport* tester, Reinhard Seiffert, began his report of the test of the S model. At the heart of the special edition was the boxer engine but with output increased to 54 DIN hp @ 4200 rpm. Volkswagen had managed to install a second carburetor in the engine compartment in spite of the tight fit. "This results in the flattest air filter ever seen," said Seiffert. Top speed rose, according to the factory, to 135 km/h, which really was the lower end of the top speed range one could expect to get from this car. S models that had been well broken in could go 140 km/h on the autobahn. *Auto, Motor und Sport* even got one up to 143 km/h and accelerated from 0 to 100 km/h in 18.8 seconds.

Compared to the single carburetor model, the S had a lot of chrome on the outside as well as the S on the license plate light. On the inside, the S had a 160 km/h speedometer and new seat and trim designs. The prices caused quite a stir: the top of the line VW cost DM 6400, not one pfennig more than the previous base 1500, which was still available. It was now called the VW 1500N and only cost DM 5990. The magazine *Mot* ran a two-year test of the VW 1500S. After 35,000 km, they reported on the car. They weren't that impressed with handling ("during critical situations often requires an unreasonable amount of driver experience and control"), lack of easy maintenance ("very difficult to set the two carburetors, which will be a problem for some shops"), the automatic choke ("good cold starts, but idle is either too fast or uneven"), the noise level

Above: The sedan cost DM 6400, the wagon cost DM 300 more. The money was definitely invested wisely.

Below: In 1963, the wagon was available as a "city delivery van" with a large cargo area covered with a rubber mat and without rear side windows.

The "city delivery van" based on the wagon.

("particularly bothersome in the lower gears"), fuel economy ("requires super fuel . . . fuel economy drops severely during short trips in the winter"), or the costs ("trips to the garage cost an amazing amount, the VW 1500S . . . is no longer a true Volkswagen" (that is, a car for the people).

Besides VW's typical strong points (build quality, operating costs, dealer network and resale value), design and ergonomics were other advantages ("operation, instruments, and instrument panel design"), as well as equipment ("does not need extra seat covers") and acceleration and performance ("no particular problems during daily driving or at full throttle on the autobahn"). In spite of these positive remarks, the VW 1500S didn't really have the best reputation. This was especially true for the people who bought the car thinking they had bought a true sports car, which the VW 1500 definitely was not, and who pushed the engine above 5000 rpm for long periods, which led some to damage the engine beyond repair. The testers from the consumer magazine *DM* managed to do just this during their 50,000 km comparison test of cars in the 1.0-liter class. This included the VW as well as Alfa Romeo Giulia 1600 TI, BMW 1500, Fiat 1500, Opel Rekord 1700, Ford 17 M 1700 and Peugeot 404. To quote from issue 10 on March 5, 1964, "We give up. We have taken the VW 1500S out of the test." According to the magazine they had major engine damage eight times, which was, in their opinion, due to a "third cylinder design flaw." Volkswagen reacted with a lawsuit, "The valve damage on the third cylinder in their VW 1500S indicates that the engine was intentionally destroyed by reckless driving." That the VW was "not reliable" and "not recommended" was something the courts were soon to deal with in the following cases:

- VW versus *DM* (temporary injunction, sued for retraction and damages),
- *DM* versus VW lawyer Augstein (a brother of the publisher of the magazine *Der Spiegel* sued for discriminating statements),

Model: VW1500 wagon
Built: 1962-63
Engine: 4 cylinder, boxer
Valves:
ohv, central camshaft
Displacement: 1493 cm^3
Bore x stroke: 83 x 69 mm
DIN hp (kW) @ rpm:
45 (33) @ 3800
Drive: rear wheels
Carburetion: 1 Solex 32 PHN
Transmission: 4F, 1R
Brakes: Drums f + r
Top speed: 130 km/h
Curbweight: 910 kg
Tires: 6.00-15
Wheelbase: 2400 mm
Track f/r: 1310/1346 mm
L x W x H:
4225 x 1605 x 1475 mm

- *DM* versus the judges of the district court of Hanover (due to bias),
- The chief justice of the district court of Hanover versus *DM* (libel),
- *DM* versus "Mot" ("[*DM*] has young drivers in uproar"; libel and slander),
- *DM* versus *Bild* (newspaper) (temporary injunction, because the newspaper had "warned" people about *DM*),
- *Bild* versus *DM* (temporary injunction against the statement that the *Bild* test "came from Porsche and VW"),
- Private lawsuit of the *Bild* testers against the publisher of *DM* (libel and defamation of character).

This was basically everyone against everyone else. At the end of it all, the provincial high court and court of appeal in Celle came to the conclusion the engine damage had been caused by revving the engine too high. "The owner's manual is explicit enough about the danger of not shifting in time and clearly indicates when to shift between gears."

Slalom Test in Sicily

The test team of the magazine *hobby* also spent a large amount of time testing the VW 1500S. In their "super test," they tested the new VW against the DKW F 102 and the Ford 17 M. The test took place in Sicily with the cars being driven along the Targa Florio route. The mountain test ("very sporty, steering direct" . . . excellent torque coming out of curves") was followed by a test on a blocked off track near Segesta ("the liveliest car, great to shift and loves to accelerate . . . tends to oversteer severely; engine very noisy"). The test crew then headed to Mount Aetna ("Definitely the fastest, load on the chassis hardly noticeable . . . but where are the four VW passengers going to store their luggage?").

The slalom test took place at a former airport near Trapazini and created an unexpected event: the VW was turned hard to the right, both inner tires came off the ground and the VW tipped on its side "as if in slow motion." The test driver climbed out of the open sunroof. The VW 1500S was put back on its feet and the test was run again. Again the VW came off the ground, but this time the driver was prepared and could shift his weight to the other side and keep all four wheels on the ground. The editors were confused and so were the engineers in Wolfsburg at first "There has never been a known incident when a car tipped over during the "slalom." Back in Stuttgart, the *hobby* editors found an answer: the incident was caused by torsion bars that were too high in conjunction with a high-friction surface. Correctly set, there was no danger of a tipover, even in a sharp curve to the right." If you are sitting alone in the VW 1500 and you have to make a quick maneuver to avoid

Model:
VW 1500S Limousine
Built: 1963-65
Engine: 4 cylinder, boxer
Valves:
ohv, central camshaft
Displacement: 1493 cm^3
B x H: 83 x 69 mm
DIN hp (kW) @ min:
54 (40) @ 4200
Drive: rear wheels
Carburetion:
2 x Solex 32 PDSIT
Transmission: 4F, 1R
Brakes: drums f + r
Top speed: 140 km/h
Curb weight: 880 kg
Tires: 6.00-15
Wheelbase: 2400 mm
Track f/r: 1310/1346 mm
L x W x H:
4225 x 1605 x 1475 mm

Torsion bars too high: During a test by *hobby*, the 1500S tipped over. The VW tipped very seldom for customers, but this situation definitely caused a lot of concern: VW's renowned reliability could have done without this direct knock.

something, turning the wheel to the left is better than turning it to the right." Customers didn't let this take away the fun of a VW 1500S. At times, 90% of Type 3 customers chose the S version of VW's mid-size car.

Two years after the much-discussed sport VW (that really was not that sporty) was introduced, it was replaced. The successor was the 1600TL, which was a completely different car in every respect.

VW 1600 (1966-74)

In the 1967 model year, the VW 1500A became the VW 1600A. The difference between the two was basically the installation of the 1.6-liter engine from the TL, except that in the A version it only had one carburetor. Output remained at 45 DIN hp. At the same time the A was introduced, Volkswagen introduced the L version with the dual-carbureted engine used in the TL. The Type 3 was now also available with an automatic transmission with torque converter and planetary gears, a concession for the US market. The new option was so popular that by the end of the decade, one out of four new VWs came off the assembly line with an automatic transmission. Also standard for the 1968 model year were a dual-circuit brake system and a safety steering column.

The most important model changes and improvements VW 1500:

1961: September, presented at the IAA, four-seater Cabriolet built by Karmann was shown but never sold.

From engine number 0001573: modified distributor.

October, carburetor modifications.

November, engine compartment cover heat-insulated.

1962: February, production of wagon begins.

May, sedan available with optional steel crank sunroof. Modified transmission.

July, modified crankcase ventilation.

August, engine modifications: larger exhaust valves, larger intake pipe; cylinders now with 14 cooling fins (previously 12), compression now 7.8 (previously 7.2); camshaft with flatter cams.

Aluminum crankshaft main bearings; clutch diameter 200 mm (previously 180 mm); wider rear brake linings (45 mm instead of 40 mm).

Wagon: optional M package with increased cargo weight from 375 kg to 460 kg, 6.00-15 6 PR ties, and equalizing springs on the rear axle.

September, 32 PHN-1 carburetor, different nozzles.

November, new rear insignia : "VW 1500."

December, modifications to lower trailing links meant different camber and toe-in settings.

1963: January, smaller crankshaft pulley; shorter belt. Heater damper housings insulated with asbestos.

February, modified pistons and piston rings.

March, maintenance-free front ball joints; number of grease nipples reduced from 8 to 4; improved windshield defrosting; sturdier glove compartment cover.

April: Fuel line relocated; front seatback now locked in place; optional Eberspächer parking heater installed in the front trunk (sedan and wagon).

May, carburetor modifications; trunk floor with special cover plate (heat insulation). Split cylinder jacket, oil cooler and cylinder sleeve could be removed without first being disassembled.

In the fall of 1967, the 54 DIN hp engines bound for the US came with a fuel-injection system instead of the two Solex carburetors available in Germany starting in May 1968; the system cost DM 580. The price also included a control module installed in the rear and covered by the fender, that used transistors and diodes to determine the fuel-air mixture ratio and control the electromagnetic injectors. Four injectors, one for each cylinder, were installed. Two

1963: July, carburetor modifications.

August, VW 1500 becomes the VW 1500N with simplified equipment level: painted window frames (previously: chrome), rear windows no longer pop out. Dropped: Bumper overriders, parking lights, door lock on right, side armrests and rear center armrest, door pockets, right sun visor, clock, and interval wipers. Sill trims also dropped, as well as locking function for front seatbacks, headlight flasher, switch panel, and left rear ashtray. No side trim or lighting for rear cargo area. New distributor, larger rear brake drums (248.1 mm instead of 231.1 mm); heat regulated via two levers between front seats. Accelerator pedal modified. Price reduced to DM 5990 (Wagon: DM 6390).

Introduction of VW 1500S: 54 DIN dual-carbureted engine. Chrome handle on front trunk, new turn signal design,side trim, parking lights lower, wheel trims, modified taillights, partially chrome-plated license plate light. For certain markets, lower compression for S engine resulting in reduced output (52 DIN hp). S wagon: standard right outside mirror.

September, carburetor modifications; flatter steel crank sunroof; heating system modified.

1964: April, 1500S with electromagnetic idle jet; fuel line relocated to reduce likelihood of vapor lock at high temperatures. Stronger valve springs; pull knobs instead of push buttons.

August, 1500N now also available with S package. Larger intake valve clearance, horn on bumper no longer below body. New bearings for rocker shafts. Curb weight now 910 kg (with GVWR: 1310 kg).

Wagon: weights 1025 kg/1400 kg.

1500S: new distributor; new carburetors; leaf valve in fuel supply line to carburetors.

October, additional heat exchanger for improved heating.

1965: April, slightly larger wheel arches (to avoid scraping of wheels when turned all the way to one side). 1500 vehicles experimentally equipped with pressed/bonded brake liners.

August, VW 1500S replaced by VW 1600TL; VW 1500N becomes the VW 1500A.

1966: August, VW 1500A replaced by VW 1600A.

injectors opened with each rotation of the crankshaft. Bosch had been working on this indirect intake manifold injection system since 1959. It was called an indirect system, because fuel was injected into the respective intake channel and not directly into the cylinder. Output did not increase, but CO emissions did decrease considerably. The percentage of unburned hydrocarbons in the exhaust dropped to 1% and even met the strict California emissions standards. Displacement, output and torque were the same as the carbureted version. A positive side effect was the improved fuel economy. The factory promised up to 2 mpg more, but tests done by the automobile press indicated this wasn't quite the case, *Auto, Motor und Sport* came up with 18.8 mpg for the carbureted 1600, while the fuel injected engine got 19.6 mpg. Performance differences were small: 0-100 km/h in 18.4 seconds (fuel-injected engine) and 18.7 seconds (carbureted engine); 1 km from a standing start 38.5 seconds compared to 38.8 seconds. Top speed was 140 km/h to 141 km/h. In comparison, a test at the end of 1965 had a VW 1600 up to 145 km/h.

The US models weren't the only ones to reap the benefits of the model improvements made to the Type 3 models in 1970 due to the US safety laws. The new 1600 was longer than its predecessor. The front was extended by 120 mm, and the shape of the car definitely changed. Few people probably noticed the similarity to the VW 411/412 as these two models weren't all that popular. The large three-chamber taillights were new (and more easily

Model: VW 1600 Limousine
Built: 1969-73
Engine: 4 cylinder, boxer
Valves:
ohv, central camshaft
Displacement: 1584 cm^3
Bore x stroke: 85.5 x 69 mm
DIN hp (kW) @ rpm:
54 (40) @ 4000
Drive: rear wheels
Carburetion:
2 Solex 32 PDSIT
Transmission: 4F, 1R
Brakes:
front discs, rear drums
Top speed: 140 km/h
Curbweight: 920 kg
Tires: 6.00-15
Wheelbase: 2400 mm
Track f/r: 1310/1346 mm
L x W x H:
4368 x 1640 x 1470 mm

The Type 3 models were very popular in the export markets and were even built in Brazil.

visible). The car was pre-wired for reverse lights, but they cost DM 30 extra. The square front turn signals were much larger and ran from the front around the side. The year before, in 1969, all vehicles (not just the automatic) got the double-jointed rear axle. This was what the Type 3 models had until production ended in July 1973. They were really no longer modern. A test report from December 1969 says it all, "In spite of the new technology installed (*Auto, Motor und Sport* had tested a fuel-injected car with automatic transmission) it is obvious that the only advantages of the VW 1600 are its reliability and high material and build quality. It's too bad that the advanced components are used to cover the inadequacy of the vehicle and engine design."

VW 1600TL

Left: The VW 1600L replaced the S model in 1965. There were no complaints about this model. This was finally a Type 3 that was a true Volkswagen: solid, safe, and reliable.

VW called the successor of the 1500S the TL (Tourenlimousine = touring sedan). Production of the TL started after the factory vacation in the late summer of 1965. This was the first time that German buyers could buy a fastback sedan of VW quality, "With the VW 1600TL, Volkswagen admitted that they had made a mistake. This mistake was the body of the VW 1500," said *Auto, Motor und Sport* laconically. Out of the honest, unassuming sedan (which had

seemed a bit outdated even at its introduction) had come a modern sporty car. The test report mentioned above explained, "The 1600TL looks like a Porsche with the passenger compartment moved too far forward." The factory, on the other hand, said, "Compared to the previous sedan, the roof on the new model slopes from the rear pillar down toward the taillights. Below that is a 300 mm high vertical skirt where the license plate is attached. Below the large sloping rear window is the trunk lid that swings upward. The modification to the rear increases luggage capacity from 200 liters to about 290 liters."

The round fastback shape didn't only bring advantages. Tests at the time indicated the car was more sensitive to sidewinds, had a poor view to the rear, and was rear-heavy when filled with cargo.

The most important mechanical innovation was the new engine with 1584 cu cm (bore x stroke: 85.5 x 69 mm, VW 1500: 83 x 69 mm). Output was the same at 54 DIN hp. Volkswagen had reduced the compression to 7.7:1. The maximum torque (11.2 mkg) was available as low as 2000 rpm. The engine in the 1500S produced 10.8 mkg at 2200 rpm. Maximum power was available at 4000 rpm; its predecessor needed 200 rpm more to reach maximum output. Basically this meant the TL was more powerful in the lower rpm ranges. This was the perfect recipe for city traffic that was getting heavier and heavier. The 1600 also was more sparing with fuel than the 1500S, which required super, while the TL used regular. The fastback VW was a part of the VW model line until the end of the 1973 model year even if it never really made a breakthrough, although at DM 6690 (1966 model year) it was several hundred less than the competition.

The last big visual changes to the model came in the 1970 model year. The front end grew by 12 cm (and the trunk volume to 8.1 cu. ft.). Larger front and rear turn signals were also installed.

Model: VW 1600TL
Built: 1965-69
Engine: 4 cylinder, boxer
Valves:
ohv, central camshaft
Displacement: 1584 cm^3
Bore x stroke: 85.5 x 69 mm
DIN hp (kW) @ rpm:
54 (40) @ 4000
Drive: rear wheels
Carburetion: 2 Solex PDSIT
Transmission: 4F, 1R
Brakes: front disc, rear drum
Top speed: 140 km/h
Curbweight: 920 kg
Tires: 6.00-15
Wheelbase: 2400 mm
Track f/r: 1310/1346 mm
L x W x H:
4368 x 1640 x 1470 mm

TL (Tourenlimousine - touring sedan) was what the Type 3 with fastback and 54 DIN hp available between 1965 and 1973 was called.

The most important model changes and improvements VW 1600TL:

1966: August, introduction of VW 1600A (sedan, 45 DIN hp) and 1600L (sedan, 54 DIN hp). Also available, a 1600 wagon. All models: 12-volt electrical system, modified distributor, more powerful generator (105 mm-diameter instead of 90 mm). 12 instead of 10 fuses, new wiring. Heat actuation via lever (as in Type 1), equalizing springs on rear axle, softer rear torsion springs.

October, cast iron brake discs, previously tempered cast.

1967: February, new crankshaft with two oil channels to the connecting rod bearings. August, introduction of an automatic transmission together with a double-joint rear axle. Torsion bars 50 mm longer, modified shock absorbers. Reinforced front end (crush zone). Dual-circuit brake system, safety steering column. Tank filler cap on the outside. Mounting points for three-point seat belts, soft plastic control knobs. Shorter hand brake lever, larger mirror on the door. Snap-off rearview mirror, outer door handles with integral release. Rotary knob for quarter vents.

Wagon: modified hatch, different license plate light. L package available at extra cost.

US models: sequential fuel injection (Bosch), exhaust emission control system (standard).

1968: May, fuel injection also available for German models (optional).

August, double-joint rear axle for all models. Standard hazard lights.

1969: February, carburetor modifications.

August, facelift: front end extended by 120 mm, rear with larger taillights. Reinforced bumpers. Vehicles with automatic transmission now approved for use with trailers. Modifications to fuel injection and carburetor.

1970: March, laminated windshield standard.

April, modifications to automatic transmission.

August, forced ventilation standard. Parking light switch connected to ignition switch. Diagnostic connector in engine compartment, larger brake lights, front and rear tow lugs. Washer fluid reservoir now 1.6 liters; wiper system modified. Wipers now park on right instead of left. Larger oil pump. Crankcase made of new alloy as in Beetle. Larger air baffles under cylinders, chrome-plated exhaust valves. Automatic transmission range indicator illuminated.

L models: better equipment with two-speed electric ventilation fan, reverse lights, trip odometer, lockable glove compartment, day/night rearview mirror.

TL: Rear trunk 20% larger, rear shelf stepped.

54 DIN hp engine: modified oil-bath air filter, dual compensator in intake manifold. Carburetor modifications.

1971: January, modified high-beam signal switch.

August, modifications to automatic transmission; front disc brakes from the Type 411. Improved door locks, larger outside door handle depression. New steering wheel with impact plate. Wipers and washer switch now on steering wheel. Chrome-plated exhaust trim dropped. Screw-type fuel tank cap.

Wagon: reinforced rear hatch lock with safety latch.

L/TL: 54 DIN engine with 7.5:1 compression (previously 7.7).

1972: January, parking light switch operates front and taillights, separate parking lights dropped.

June, new seats with improved anchoring.

August, modified armrests and transmission. Engine oil drain plug dropped.

1973: July, production of VW 1600 ends.

VW Karmann-Ghia 1500/1600 (1961-69)

The Karmann-Ghia 1500/1600 was the first Volkswagen to be taken out of the model line after only eight years. Internally this car was known as the Type 34, the fourth Type variation after sedan, convertible and wagon that was to be added to the line.

The complete Type 3 family was introduced at the IAA in September 1961, together with a Karmann-Ghia Cabriolet (that never actually entered production). Seventeen of them were built between 1961 and 1963, all test cars. Karmann has one of them. At least one of the others survived and is owned by a private collector.

The deep rear window was a hot topic for debate as it was a quite unusual style at the time. The luxury L package included two door pockets, a second ashtray, parking lights, chrome-plated exhaust trim and other extras.

Above:
Metal puzzle:
TL bodies-in-white.

Above right:
To meet the US safety regulations, VW had to install seats with headrests starting in 1972. Seats with a solid, non-adjustable headrest were called "tombstones" in the US. These were only available at extra cost in Germany.

Below right:
1971 model year: reverse lights, two-speed fan and a modified wiper system were standard as well as a lockable glove compartment, trip odometer and a mirror in the passenger sun visor.

Ghia had again designed this "large" Karmann. Sergio Sartorelli had drawn it up as early as 1958. The Turin design magicians created a completely new, more aggressive car that was in stark contrast to the round, almost feminine Ghia 1200. The new body was balanced, with the long nose harmonizing with the softly sloping rear. The elegant roof with its delicate lines and the large windows provided the car with a feeling of elegance and luxury. The near-vertical windshield and sharply sloping rear window created a much different car than the coupes of other European manufacturers. The closest resemblance was to the Chevrolet Corvair; in particular the rear area.

The Karmann-Ghia Type 34 was wider, longer, and higher with a curb weight of 893 kg (900 kg for the 1600), which was 80 kg heavier than the "smaller" Karmann. While the latter had a wider floor pan (compared to the Beetle), underneath the chic metal of the

Type 34 was true Type 3 technology. The amount of interior space between the sedan and coupe was basically the same (the shoulder width of 126 cm in the front was 1 cm more than in the sedan, and 2 cm more than the Ghia 1200). Headroom was also almost identical between the coupe and sedan (the Ghia offered .05 cm more).

The Ghia seats, on the other hand, were lower and about 10 cm deeper. Most drivers were forced to push their seat far back (the seats could be adjusted 120 mm forwards and backwards) and assume the classic "Italian" sports car driver position, with extended arms. This was tiring after a while, and the shift lever wasn't as close at hand. However, in that position it was possible to open the rear vent windows, which made drivers happy as the ventilation was totally inadequate. The Type 34 at least had quarter vents in the front, which did help ventilation. This was something the "smaller" model didn't have. Otherwise there was little else to complain about. The controls were close at hand. Three large instruments were located directly in front of the driver: fuel gauge on the left with indicator lights for parking lights and high beams, generator, oil pressure and turn signals, a speedometer in the center and a clock on the right. The rocker switch for the standard fog lights was located underneath the instrument panel. A test at

Mechanically, the Karmann-Ghia was very similar to the Type 3. The steel body built by Karmann sat on the tubular backbone frame from the sedan. The engine also came from the VW 1500. Output was the same with a top speed of 137 km/h. The Type 3 went 130 km/h.

Dashboard 1966: The surface was no longer painted in body color but covered in a woodgrain film with a Karmann-Ghia insignia. The steering wheel came from the Beetle, with a chrome horn semi-circle.

the time complained that the fog lights could only be switched on together with low beams. This was due to the fact the fog lights were located around 50 mm more toward the center of the car than was legally allowed.

Otherwise the Type 34 received only praise from the motor press around the world. The "big Karmann" was the best Volkswagen ever and the one that was the most fun to drive. The low center of gravity really helped (and was particularly useful when cornering). Otherwise there were few differences between the coupe and the sedan. Both cornered well and tended to understeer in tight curves and lightly oversteer in fast curves. The Ghia pilot usually had the sportier handling, though, compared to the driver in the sedan. Thanks to its slimmer silhouette, the Ghia wasn't as sensitive to side winds as the normal VW 1500. Steering was easy and precise enough with 2.8 turns from lock to lock. *Auto, Motor und Sport* called the shifting along with the transmission "a source of driving pleasure," with particular praise for the 3rd gear ratio, which could be used up to 110 km/h and harmonized well with the low rpm VW power plant. The fun quickly ended at the gas station. At full throttle on the autobahn (which brought the Ghia to over 135 km/h) the car got only 18.2 mpg (on super). The Ghia was definitely no longer a true "Volkswagen," not that it had ever been, especially at a cost of DM 8750 (DM 2400 more than the sedan). This meant, of course, that fewer cars would be sold. The fact that the Type 34 was not sold in the US added to this.

Seldom were test teams so unanimous: All in all the "large Karmann" was one of the best cars of all time. It was a high-quality vehicle in terms of build quality, equipment, handling, and performance but was not honored for such by buyers. By 1969, no more than 42,498 had been built.

Model: Karmann Ghia 1500S
Built: 1962-65
Engine: 4 cylinder, boxer
Valves: ohv
Displacement: 1493 cm^3
Bore x stroke: 83 x 69 mm
DIN hp (kW) @ rpm:
45 (33) @ 3800
Drive: rear wheels
Carburetion: 2 Solex 32 PDSIT
Transmission: 4F, 1R
Brakes: drums f+r
Top speed: 137 km/h
Curb weight: 910 kg
Tires: 6.00-15
Wheelbase: 2400 mm
Track f/r: 1310/1346 mm
L x W x H:
4280 x 1620 x 1335 mm

The 1500S engine with 54 DIN hp was introduced in 1963, followed by the 1600 engine in 1965. Starting in 1968, the Coupe was also available with fuel injection.

Left: Developed under the project name "Lyon": the Karmann-Ghia 1500, the "large" Karmann-Ghia.

The most important model changes and improvements Type 34:

1961-69:	same as Type 3 model S, plus the following:
1961:	September, premiere at the IAA as Coupe and Cabriolet. Mechanically same as Type 3 sedan. Base price, DM 8750, Cabriolet DM 9500. November, start of mass production of VW 1500 Karmann-Ghia as a Coupe; Cabriolet not built.
1962:	July, extra cost: electric steel sunroof; the switch for the sunroof was installed below the cigarette lighter (on the right of the clock). November, improved seatback adjustment. Adjustment wheel moved 45 mm upward, additional springs. Changes to doors (including modified quarter vents).
1963:	February, improved cooling air flow, battery ventilation via two holes each in cross-member and front rail of rear seat. May, grill over cooling air intake, covered side water drain holes. August, Karmann-Ghia 1500 Coupe only available with 54 DIN hp engine. Stronger 6.00 S 15 L tires (up to 160 km/h). Heater actuation via lever between front seats. Horn button on steering wheel (previously: semi-circle ring). Seats and lower door trim in leatherette. New steel wheels without holes; new emblem in the front (round, previously rectangular). Right-hand drive version introduced.
1964:	August, new interior colors and designs. Two-speed wipers. Optional alloy wheel rings and rear window defroster. Improved interior equipment (make-up mirror on passenger side, front carpeting instead of rubber mats).
1966:	August, locking front seatbacks; sun visor swivel point changed. Modifications to seats. Short hand brake lever and relocated shift lever. Door lock mechanism: pull handle on outside with lever on inside. Optional: wood-grain finish on dashboard.
1967:	August, seat rail anchors and front trunk latch from Type 3 sedan. Stronger wiper arms. Automatic transmission and fuel injection available, as in sedan.
1968:	August, hazard lights, modified taillights, flatter hubcaps.
1969:	July, production ends. Replaced by VW-Porsche 914.

Model: Karmann-Ghia 1600L
Built: 1965-69
Engine: 4 cylinder, boxer
Valves: ohv
Displacement: 1584 cm^3
Bore x stroke: 85.5 x 69 mm
DIN hp (kW)@ rpm:
54 (40) @ 4000
Drive: rear wheels
Carburetion:
2 Solex 32 PDSIT
Transmission: 4F, 1R
Brakes:
front discs, rear drums
Top speed: 150 km/h
Curb weight: 910 kg
Tires: 6.00-15
Wheelbase: 2400 mm
Track f/r: 1310/1346 mm
L x W x H:
4280 x 1620 x 1335 mm

EA 142, the sedan that never went into production. This one-of-a-kind built in 1966 is now in the VW museum in Wolfsburg. Its front end was used two years later in the Type 4.

Chapter 7

VW Type 4 411/412 (1968-74)

Left: This sporty version of the VW 1500 / Type 3 as a Cabriolet was only used for the IAA in September 1961. The open 2+2 never went into production.

The VW 411 was Heinrich Nordhoff's final legacy. Its air-cooled boxer engine in the rear was the only thing that reminded one of the hallowed VW tradition. Unfortunately, it was introduced during a recession, which wasn't Nordhoff's fault. The whole of German industry, from construction to automobiles, was suffering at the time (1967-68). This was due to the iintroduction of the value-added tax (VAT) and strengthening of the Mark, which led to a decrease in exports. In addition, there were more and more foreign imports coming into Germany due to the fall of several duty barriers in 1966. The market share of Italian and French imports rose to 25%. In 1960, they had only been one of every ten cars sold. The German manufacturers were under tremendous pressure. Opel laid off 6000

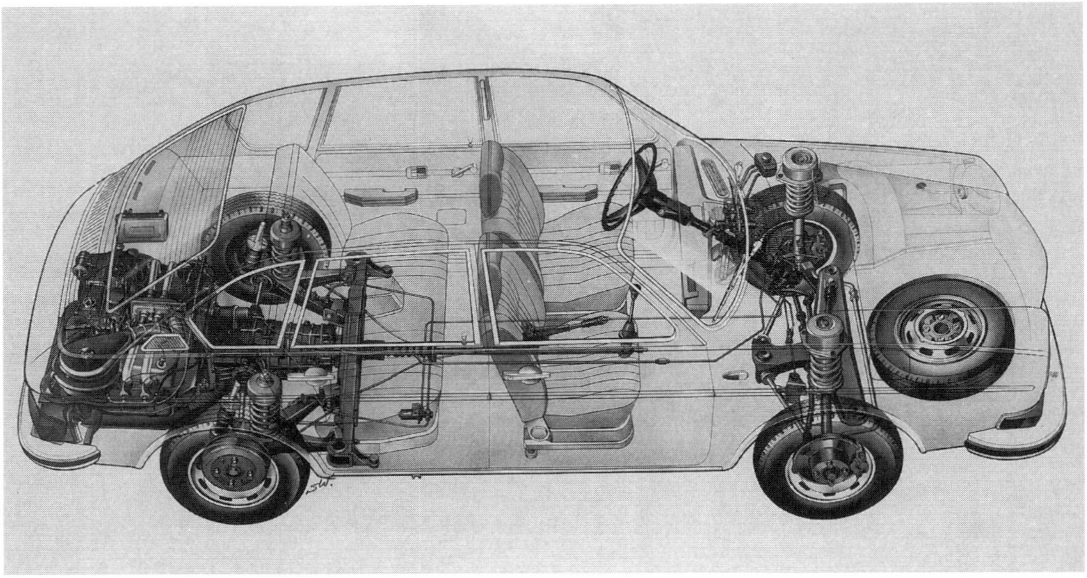

workers, while VW ordered 17 part-time days and dropped to the second-largest European automobile manufacturer behind Fiat.

The first Volkswagen passenger car with unitized construction.

The Design

The Type 4 was the first "true" sedan from VW. It had a unitized body, MacPherson struts and coil springs instead of the torsion bars, as well as a new 1.7-liter engine, which output 68 DIN hp and could hold its own against the competition. Both the sedan and the

Complicated — the new front axle: independent suspension with transverse links, struts, and stabilizer. Disc brakes were standard.

Full instrumentation: Only the L models had a clock. In the base cars, a combination dial took its place.

wagon (introduced later) had a large trunk area in the long front end, which provided the German nickname of the Type 4, the "Nasenbär"(coati). Theoretically, the car had all the ingredients necessary to become a successful family sedan. In practice, however, the shape was too unconventional and the design too modern for the car to be a great success. Volkswagen head, Heinrich Nordhoff, who died on April 12, 1968, didn't live to see the introduction of the "large Volkswagen."

The Chassis

With the Type 4, VW finally got away from the Beetle-style chassis. Instead of a trailing link front axle with torsion bars, the VW 411 had wishbones, MacPherson struts and stabilizer design. Steering was via recirculating-ball steering with three-part tie rods and safety steering column. The rear axle, when introduced, was not necessarily the newest design, but compared to the other rear engine models, it was a complete overhaul. A double-jointed rear axle was still used, but the torsion bars were replaced by double-acting telescopic shock absorbers and progressive rubber springs. Compared to the swing-arm axle in the Beetle, this design resulted in much more neutral cornering, as toe-in and camber only changed slightly

Improvements after only ten months: with electronic fuel injection the 1.7-liter engine output 80 DIN hp. The model was now the 411E.

in relation to suspension movements. A stabilizer was also installed on the rear axle starting in the 1970 model year.

The Engine

The air-cooled boxer engine had 1679 cm^3 displacement and output 68 DIN hp at 4500 rpm. Maximum torque was 124.5 Nm at 2800 rpm. The crankcase of the first generation Type 4 was made of a magnesium alloy. The forged crankshaft rotated in four main friction bearings with hardened bearing housings. The flywheel was bolted to the head of the crankshaft using five bolts. The connecting rods ran in bronze bearings, with the wrist pins floating in bronze bushings. The pistons were made of alloy, with the cylinder barrels made of gray cast iron. These barrels could be replaced individually but each pair used a single alloy cylinder head. The overhead valve actuation was via rocker arms and alloy push rods. Carburetion was via two Solex PDSIT downdraft carburetors with 34-mm intake and an electrically heated automatic choke. The fuel pump was driven by an eccentric on the camshaft and was installed directly on the engine. The air filter was an oil-bath and was connected to the caburetors via a flat, wide air conduit.

The engine was a long-stroke design (the bore of 90 mm and stroke of 66 mm was typical for a VW engine). This wasn't a super-powered racing engine but a reliable workhorse designed to run for tens of thousands of kilometers with a wide usable rpm range (between 1800 and 3900 rpm). The new four-speed transmission with remote shift was together in one unit with the engine. The gearbox itself and final drive were in the same housing. The helical-cut gears were continuously engaged; pinion and crown wheel were hypoid gears.

The VW 411 was available with two and four doors. Both came with a rear engine which provided certain advantages in the winter.

VW 411 (1968-72)

"The Beetle grew and grew and grew and when it was big enough it was called the 411." These were the words used by *Auto, Motor und Sport* to introduce the fastest Volkswagen to date (148 km/h).

Nasenbär (the "nosebear"): According to the measurements by a German automobile magazine, the trunk in the Type 4 held 13.6 cu. ft., around three times as large as the Beetle's.

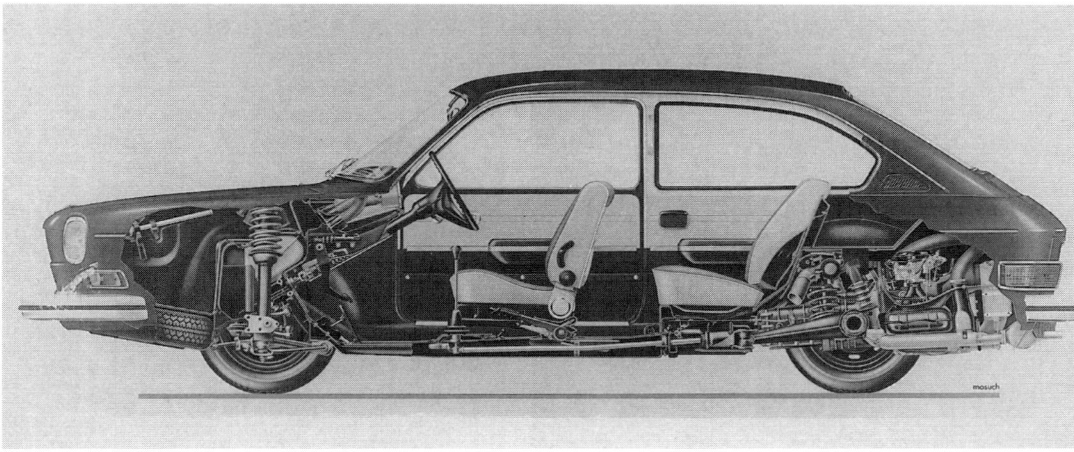

Typical VW: engine in the rear, trunk in the front.

The sarcastic writers, on the other hand, had other words to describe this car: four doors, eleven years too late. This hit on the problem directly. The Type 4 was better than its reputation; its ancestry was the problem. As a product from VW, the 411 was expected to behave just as its predecessors, the Type 1 and Type 3.

When measured against this, the early Type 4 cars were lacking in some departments. But the Type 3, in particular the S version, also had some growing pains when it was first introduced, and it took a long, careful process of model improvements to reach adulthood. The Type 4 wasn't given enough time to mature. After only six years and 370,000 units, it disappeared from the model line in 1974.

Everything had started so nicely. The first cars were delivered to the dealers on October 5, 1968; the "large Volkswagen" was finally here. The car was almost 4.6 m long (noticeably longer than the VW 1600). The VW Type 4 had a 10 cm longer wheelbase than the Type 1 or Type 3 cars. With the 2500 mm wheelbase this VW had every right to call itself a mid size sedan.

The car looks "very high quality," according to *Der Spiegel* (issue 33/1968), which was present at the dealer introduction to the car in Brunswick. Others saw "every reason to get drunk after getting excited by the car." Nordhoff's legacy seemed to be the car to keep those wanting to trade up from the Beetle in the VW camp. This excitement didn't last for very long. The best month for the Type 4 was October with 4607 buyers. In November, 3164 were sold, and in December, 2897. By the end of the year, VW dealers had sold 11,000 Type 4s and very few buyers were former Opel or Ford customers as the marketing people had expected. The new shape wasn't as popular as was originally thought. *Auto, Motor und Sport* criticized the front end ("much too long . . . lifeless lines . . . headlights not integrated well into body") and wasn't alone. *Der Spiegel* called the design "a muddle." Even Nordhoff's successor. Lotz, admitted that this wasn't a "metal Adonis." The VW boss did

Left:
The "large Volkswagen," wasn't the success its creators had hoped. This was definitely not due to the interior: it was solid, well-built and practical. The front seats in the L package even reclined.

The most important model changes and improvements in the Type 411:

1968: August, production of VW 411 starts (as two- and four-door). Air-cooled 1.7-liter boxer engine with dual-carburetor system and 68 DIN hp @ 4500 rpm. Front struts with stabilizer, semi-trailing arm rear axle. Four-speed manual transmission, optional automatic. Gasoline-electrical auxiliary heater standard; could be used as a parking heater. Standard 155 SR 15 tires, alternator.

L package: Carpeting instead of rubber mats, reclining seats with lumbar support, velour seat covers. Pockets in seatbacks.

October, first cars delivered. Insulation mats for wheel housings installed in engine compartment (noise insulation).

1969: January, engine modifications (intake and exhaust channels, rocker arm changes). Heater boxes relocated in front of rear axle on the body (noise reduction measure). Heater ducts altered. Modifications to transmission and rear axle (to prevent rumbling noises). Enlarged front door openings. Clutch driven plate torsion-spring to prevent judder. Insulation mats under rear seat and fire wall.

August, introduction of the VW 411E: Bosch fuel injection, higher compression, modified cylinder heads and distributor. Aluminum pressure-cast engine block and oil pan. Engine supported in four mounts (previously three). Oil filler neck and dipstick higher. Double halogen headlights.

All models: VW insignia with trim strip on front lid, silver steel wheels. Seating position lower, improved seats, instruments more deeply recessed, larger ashtray, side armrests without trim strip. Continuously variable fresh-air fan, larger air extraction slits under the rear window. Improved noise insulation. L package includes cigarette lighter. Stabilizer on the rear axle.

Carbureted models: Wide-beam headlights instead of ovals. Optional automatic transmission. Introduction of the 411E wagon: only available with two doors and hatch. Rear foldable seat. Exhaust outlets in C pillar. Different rear axle ratio, 165 SR 15 tires. Optional: speedometer with trip odometer and clock. Air conditioning with center vent.

September, more powerful alternator.

October, tail pipe moved to right on E models.

1970: March, front castor increased from 9 to 16 mm by relocating the steering knuckle.

April, shorter shift rod, new selector finger mechanism.

August, front hood with designated fold line and catch hooks, to prevent (as much as possible) the windshield from getting crushed in a crash. Tow hooks in the front and rear. Threaded tank filler cover with overtightening protection. Interior modifications: black dash (previously wood-grain imitation); steering lock with lock cylinder, door knobs in the window frames, seat rails with extra side reinforcements (US standard); control switch for auxiliary heater located on dashboard, floor lever on left dropped. Parking heater switched off after ten minutes to protect the battery. Increased valve clearances, automatic now available in E model. Idle rpm regulator. Headlights only on if ignition also on. Central diagnostic connector in engine compartment. US models: activated charcoal filter for fuel tank ventilation.

1971: August, door locks reinforced including push buttons in door handles. Four-spoke steering wheel with crash pad. Wiper and washer switch on steering wheel at right. 190 km/h speedometer. New ignition distributor, modified crankcase ventilation, split rear engine cover. Larger muffler cover plate. Screen over oil pump intake. Pre-heated intake air. Optional: power brake booster.

1972: July, modified rear axle ratio (sedan).

August, introduction of VW 412.

Model: 411 sedan
Built: 1968-69
Engine:
4 cylinder boxer, air-cooled
Valves:
ohv, central camshaft
Displacement: 1679 cm³
Bore x stroke: 90 x 66 mm
DIN hp (kW) @ rpm:
68 (50) @ 4500
Drive: rear wheels
Carburetion: 2 x Solex 34 PDSIT carburetors
Transmission: 4 F, 1 R
Brakes:
front discs, rear drums
Top speed: 145 km/h
Curb weight: 1020 kg (2-door)
Tires: 155 SR 15
Wheelbase: 2500 mm
Track f/r: 1376/1342 mm
L x W x H:
4525 x 1635 x 1485 mm

think, though, that the daily production of 80 would increase considerably. VW planned to be building "considerably more than 500" a day in 1969.

The fact that fewer cars were sold than planned was in part due to the lack of Type 4 model variety. The sedan (with two or four doors) was only available as a fastback (a shape that hadn't been very popular when used for the VW 1600). The wagon was available a year later, but only as a two-door. In addition to the lack of variety came the less than euphoric test reports. *Mot*, for example, criticized (as others did) the unbelievably annoying noise level (which was even higher than that in the Beetle or Type 3) and the rumbling noises from the rear axle. There were also positive things about the car. "It is attractive and well-equipped, offering four passengers plenty of room. Build quality is good. When cornering it is neutral or understeers lightly." (*Auto, Motor und Sport*).

The reputation of the car was also affected by the wide variation in engines used. Only a few people were able to get the 68 DIN hp engine that had been announced. After less than a year, this 1.7-liter carbureted engine was modified with the inclusion of a Bosch fuel injection system. Output in this E model was increased to 80 DIN hp, which put the 411 ahead of the competition (Opel Rekord, Ford 17 M and Audi 75).

411E / Wagon (1969-72)

The VW 411E with fuel injection had more power thanks not only to the Bosch fuel injection (used previously in the VW 1600). Modified pistons increased compression to 8.2:1. This was in addition to the modified cylinder heads with larger intake changes and intake valves, and the modified camshaft and different distributor. To strengthen the engine against the higher output, VW used an aluminum crankcase instead of a magnesium one. With this engine the "Nasenbär" (the "nosebear," as it was nicknamed) hit 155 km/h and went from 0-100 km/h in 15 seconds. The 411E was now "a VW with a shot of Porsche," according to *Mot* tester, Engelbert Männer.

VW was of this opinion as well. "That there is a VW with as much as 80 DIN hp is something. But what is even more interesting is that the engine produces this much power without straining itself." But what was really the most interesting (something the VW ads failed to mention) was that the VW 411 was now available as a wagon, the best way to drive a Type 4. For the new wagon, Wolfsburg came up with the term "Grossraumlimousine" (minivan), a word they also used for the 1600 wagon. At the time, buyers didn't know what that term really meant. In 1969, 400,000 wagons were sold in Germany; most of them were company cars or for workmen. The best-selling wagon was the Opel Rekord Caravan, followed by the Ford Turnier and the VW 1600 wagon.

During the first few months it was sold, the wagon was chosen by 50% of the Type 4 buyers. This was only 5% of the total VW sales, though. According to the marketing experts, the wagon should be 30% of sales. In actuality, the share rose to above 60%. What they hadn't expected though was that most of the wagon buyers had been Beetle and 1600 owners. This is why *Mot* compared the advantages and disadvantages of the 411 against the competition as well as against the VW 1600. Compared to the latter, the 411 wagon was a huge step forward. Engine output, safety, driving comfort and space were much better. The heaviness of the rear and the hard-to-see deep inset instruments were worse. Compared to the competition, the results were much worse: the wagon was uncomfortable, as only available with two doors, sensitive to sidewinds, loud, hard to drive at first and weak.

Model: 411E / wagon
Built: 1969-72
Engine:
4 cylinder boxer, air-cooled
Valves:
ohv, central camshaft
Displacement: 1679 cm3
Bore x stroke: 90 x 66 mm
DIN hp (kW) @ rpm:
80 (58) @ 4900
Drive: rear wheels
Fuel injection:
Bosch fuel injection
Transmission: 4 F, 1 R
Brakes:
front discs, rear drums
Top speed: 155 km/h
Curb weight: 1100 kg
Tires: 155 SR 15/165 SR 15
Wheelbase: 2500 mm
Track f/r: 1376/1342 mm
L x W x H:
4525 x 1635 x 1485 mm

412E / Wagon (1972-74)

For the 1973 model year VW decided to give the Type 4 a comprehensive facelift. With this change, VW rebadged the car. This was done to tell people that the car had really changed and this was a much better Type 4. The VW 412 got a redesigned front end, still with the unconventional shape though. Changes under the hood came in the 1974 model year. The 1.7-liter engine was dropped and in its place came two 1.8-liter engines with 75 and 85 DIN hp. The increased displacement was due to the 3-mm increase in cylinder bore. VW used this opportunity to drop the troublesome electronic fuel injection and went back to carburetors. The 75 DIN hp engine used in the N model had a compression of 7.8, while the 85 DIN hp engine in the S model had a compression of 8.6. Top power output

Model: 412 sedan (2-door)
Built: 1973-74
Engine:
4 cylinder boxer, air-cooled
Valves:
ohv, central camshaft
Displacement: 1795 cm^3
Bore x stroke: 93 x 66 mm
DIN hp (kW) @ rpm:
75 (55) @ 5000
Drive: rear wheels
Carburetion: 2 x Solex 40 PDSIT carburetors
Transmission: 4 F, 1 R
Brakes:
front discs, rear drums
Top speed: 150 km/h
Curb weight: 1080 kg (2-door)
Tires: 155 SR 15/165 SR 15
Wheelbase: 2500 mm
Track f/r: 1386/1350 mm
L x W x H:
4555 x 1675 x 1475 mm

came at 5000 rpm in both engines, with maximum torque at 3400 rpm. In terms of acceleration and top speed, the engines were very similar, with the S engine a bit faster (top speed was close to 160 km/h). The N model went just over 150 km/h. But the weaker engine was the better choice as it used regular gasoline, while the S engine required super. The S engine also had problems with carburetion and tended to hesitate when the throttle was opened. The N engine, on the other hand, ran smoother. Whether S or N power plant, the air-cooled pushrod boxer definitely profited from the return to carburetors.

In spite of all the effort, the fuel injection was always one of the weak spots. Many shops were unable to deal with the complicated electronics, which used diodes and transistors to transfer data, such as engine temperature, rpm, intake pressure and throttle valve opening angle, to the computer. Also, the VW 412 got better fuel economy than the E model. Tests indicated an average of 17.6 mpg for the S engine, and 18.5 mpg for the N engine (around 2 mpg more than the E model).

The Type 4 was also never cheap. When introduced, the 411 wagon cost DM 8355. The L package added DM 400 to the price. The most economical VW 412L cost DM 10,995 in 1974, while the 412LS cost DM 11,145. In terms of price, the VW was alone at the top. Neither Ford nor Opel asked their clients to pay as much.

In July of 1974, the Type 4 headed for the museum and was replaced by the Passat. The wagon remained in production until the Passat wagon was introduced.

Extensive reworking of the front and rear was designed to make the "large Volkswagen" more attractive for customers in the 1973 model year. The engine had not changed.

"Not exactly an Adonis," admitted Nordhoff's successor, Kurt Lotz, in an interview about the VW 412LE, 1973 model year.

The Type 4 couldn't quite get away from its wallflower reputation. Only the wagon sold fairly well, although it was only available as a two-door model.

Production of the Type 4 ended in July 1974; 367,728 had been built. A total of 2.6 million Type 3s were built (production of that car had ended the previous year).

The most important model changes and improvements in the VW 412:

1972: August, redesigned front end and hood. Double headlights in new covers. Bumpers and turn signals higher. Only sedan: two license plate lights, higher taillights. Wagon: narrower taillights. Only two-door model: larger door openings. Black-matte wiper arms. Outside mirrors with rubber collar. Storage pockets in front doors, door armrests with hand grip in underside. Reinforced front seat mountings. Turn signal used as parking light switch with ignition off. Modified ignition timing, brake pads and stronger transmission synchromesh. Modifications to struts and stabilizer (tighter). Fuel injected models: paper air filter instead of oil-bath air filter. Pre-heating of intake air dropped.

December, push-button interior lighting.

1973 August, fuel injection replaced by dual carburetors (except for US). 1.7-liter with 68 DIN hp dropped. Displacement increased to 1795 cm^3.

Models: 412 (N engine, 75 DIN hp, regular gas) and 412S (85 DIN hp, super gasoline). US model: fuel injection and 76 DIN hp. New mufflers (Gillet), and steering track rods with stronger ball-joints. Fourth gear ratio modified. Disc wheels with 41 mm offset (increased front and rear track by 10 mm). Larger blower fan for ventilation, quartz clock, new high-beam switch. Optional: headlight washers. US models: reinforced bumpers and mounts according to new standard that bumpers return to their original position after impact.

1974 July, production ends. Wagon built until Passat wagon introduced.

Chapter 8

VW-Porsche 914 (1969-76)

The VW-Porsche 914 was designed to appeal to two types of buyers: to Karmann-Ghia owners who were looking to trade up, and to first time Porsche buyers. In spite of an excellent concept, the "people's Porsche" never made a breakthrough.

A true sports car in any age has to have concealed headlights. The VW-Porsche wasn't a true sports car in terms of performance until the introduction of the 2.0-liter four-cylinder with 100 DIN hp. Road holding was flawless thanks to the mid-engine design.

The mid-engine car came with Porsche instruments. As in a true sports car, the tachometer was right in the center of the driver's field of vision. Unfortunately, the flat engine taken from the Type 4 didn't live up to the sporty claim.

The Background History

Ten years earlier, in 1956, VW engineers had designed and built a small, open two-seater and had readied it for production until VW head, Nordhoff, stopped it from going into production. The topic was again up for debate in the autumn of 1966. Particularly in the US market, VW was lacking a sports car to boast about. VW was looking at the competition, in particular the MG B, of which 12,000 a year were sold.

Heinrich Nordhoff and Ferry Porsche decided to work together to build an affordable open two-seater. The work was divided according to a well-known pattern: Porsche developed and VW paid. To keep costs down, it was decided that as many parts as possible should come from the VW parts bin, in particular the engine and chassis. At first, the car was going to be sold only by VW. But the Porsche engineers were quite happy with the car, and they decided they also wanted to build a Porsche version of the "Roadster" (VW's internal name for the car).

The project was in the hands of Heinrich Klie, who was also responsible for the development of the Carrera 6. He drew the clean, no-frills lines of the VW-Porsche. Even his successor, Ferdinand Alexander Porsche (who had designed the Porsche 911) didn't change much on the mid-engine design. VW saw the 914 for the first time in 1967. The first prototype was ready on March 1, 1968. Production was contracted to Karmann in Osnabrück, where the Type 34 Karmann-Ghia (the "large Karmann") was also built. The official introduction of the VW sports car took place at the IAA in Frankfurt in 1969. This was the first mass-produced

914

Left:
The VW-Porsche 914 was the first mass-produced mid-engine car. It was designed to cause a sensation, particularly in the US, and make life difficult for the competition, in particular the Spiders from Fiat and Alfa.

Below:
The center roof panel could be removed, though, it was usually good to have two people do it.

the IAA in Frankfurt in 1969. This was the first mass-produced mid-engine vehicle.

VW Porsche 914/4 (1969-76)

The small mid-engine car (3.97 m long and 1.23 m high) was a two-seater designed for sportiness. This was also reflected in the price. The VW-Porsche (available in the US only as the Porsche 914) cost almost DM 12,000 and didn't quite seem to live up to that price at first glance. The center roof piece weighed 9 kg and could be easily removed, though. Under the open sky, the 914 offered a true Cabriolet experience, which helped people to forgive the somewhat sparse interior. Most buyers spent DM 600 more and ordered the "S" version. This included such goodies as chrome-plated bumpers, a black roll bar, chrome trim pieces on the wheel arches, and halogen headlights. Inside, the checkered seats were more exciting than the standard black leatherette seats. Base car or S, it didn't matter; the car was a lot of fun for any driver, "The Porsche 914 handles very well, provides excellent views, and fits you like a glove" according to *Mot. Auto, Motor und Sport* added, "The more difficult the road, the more this driving machine demonstrates how well it handles, turns, and corners."

914 1.7/1.8 (1969-76)

The base mid-engine car came with a 1.7-liter engine with 80 DIN hp. This air-cooled four-cylinder boxer engine came from the VW 411E and was equipped with a D-Jetronic fuel-injection system. Top speed was around 175 km/h and in tests, up to 180 km/h. "Not slow in any way. A real peppy car" (*Auto, Motor und Sport*), "but with just enough power to match its reputation." A minor change was made in that department in 1974, when the 1.7-liter was replaced by the 1.8-liter from the VW 412LE. For Europe, this engine was equipped with Weber twin carburetors; for the US it had Bosch L-Jetronic. The matching transmission was a VW development. The gear ratios were sufficient, but the long shift throws reduced precision somewhat. With a full tank, the 1.23 m high Targa weighed 940 kg. That it was fairly successful in tests by automobile magazines was only due to this low weight.

914/2.0 (1972-76)

The 914/2.0 appeared in the 1973 model year. It replaced the outrageously priced 914/6. In terms of performance, the 2.0-liter Porsche came quite close to the six-cylinder. Top speed was around 190 km/h, with 0-100 km/h in 10.5 seconds. This car was definitely not underpowered and could hold its own against fast Alfas, BMWs, or Capris. The new 100 DIN hp engine was based on the previous 1.7-liter fuel-injected engine. Displacement was increased by 292 cm³ by increasing the bore and modifying the crankshaft (bore: 94 mm, stroke: 71 mm). The valve covers and camshaft came from the smaller four-cylinder. The 20 DIN hp definitely helped performance. *Mot* talked about a "real power boost" and quickly got to the point: the 2.0-liter 914 was fast, solid, and relatively good value. At DM 13,760, it only cost DM 400 more than the 914/1.7 (which was still available for purchase). A modified gearshift linkage even made shifting fun. What had made the VW-Porsche such a great car up to that point—the removable roof piece, two trunks in the front and rear and the handling, were naturally retained.

When the ever increasing build quality (which had fluctuated quite a bit at the beginning) finally reached the expected high level, many people were calling the 2.0-liter VW-Porsche the best ever. Today, this isn't the most sought-after model, though. That honor belongs to the six-cylinder, which nobody wanted at the time it was built.

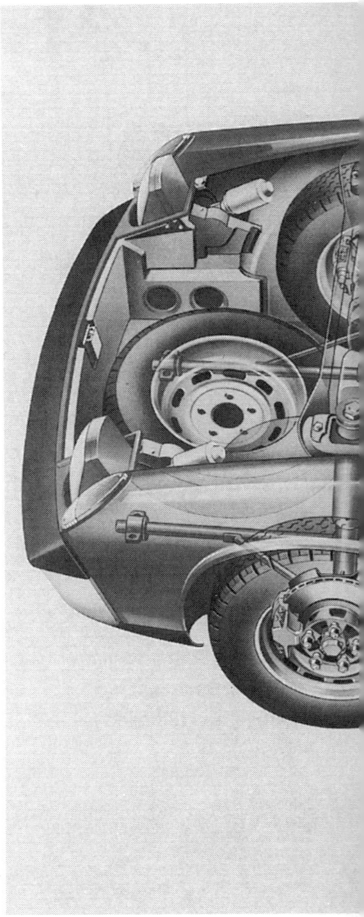

VW-Porsche 914/6 (1969-72)

A six-cylinder version (with the engine from the Porsche 911T) was introduced at the same time as the four-cylinder. The 914/6 was a true Porsche and was also built at the Porsche factory. The four-cylinder was built by Karmann, while Karmann sent bodies-in-white for the six-cylinder from their factory to the Porsche factory in Zuffenhausen for final assembly. Registrations for the six-cylinder noted Porsche as the manufacturer, while the four-cylinder noted VW.

Auto, Motor und Sport: "The high-performance chassis has a matched high-performance engine in this car." They put the sports car in a "superior position." Not much of the performance was visible from the outside. The only exterior differences between the six-cylinder and its less powerful brother were the wider tires and wheels (165 HR 15 on 5.5 J 15 Fuchs wheels), chrome-plated bumpers, and black vinyl covering the roll bar.

When driving the car, though, there was no mistaking the two. The 914 sounded like a real Porsche, with the 110 DIN hp six-cylinder from the Porsche 911T also providing the expected performance. "An aggressive voice . . . not quiet at all, but not annoying either," according to one tester. A total of only 3381 Porsche six-cylinders were built. That there weren't any more was due to the price: DM 19,000 for the 914/6, almost 50% more than the four-cylinder. The base 911, the Porsche 911T, only cost DM 999 more. The prices were just too close. The 914/6 was dropped from the model line as of the 1972 model year.

Model: 914/6
Built: 1969-72
Engine: 6-cylinder boxer
Valves: 2 x ohv
Displacement: 1991 cm³
Bore x stroke: 80 x 66 mm
DIN hp (kW) @ rpm:
110 (80) @ 5800
Drives: rear wheels
Carburetion: 2 x Weber 40 IDT
Transmission: 5F, 1R
Brakes: front and rear discs
Top speed: 201 km/h
Curb weight: 980 kg
Tires: 165 HR 15/185 HR 14
Wheelbase: 2450 mm
Track f/r: 1337/1374 mm
L x W x H:
3985 x 1650 x 1230 mm

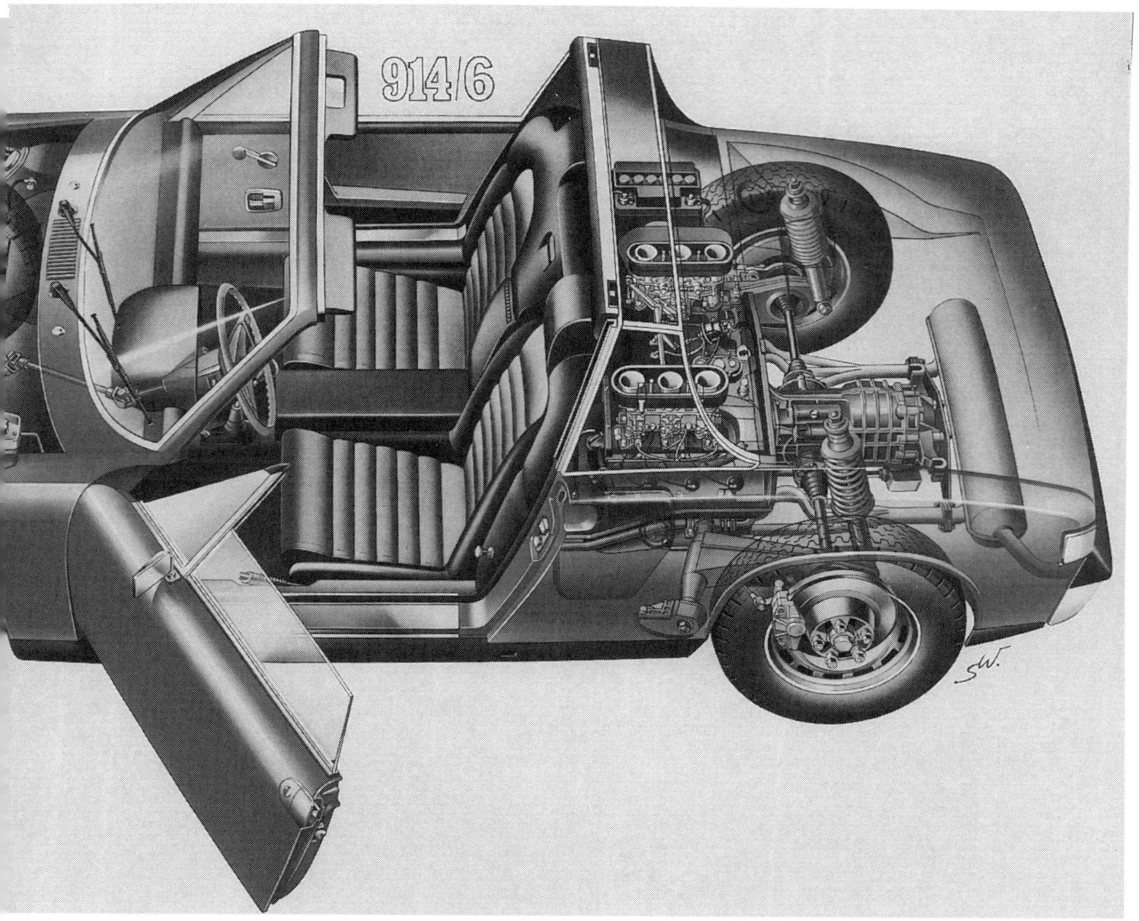

Six appeal: The 914/6 was built by Porsche in Zuffenhausen. The six-cylinder engine came from the Porsche 911. Production of the 914/6 ended in 1971 with the remaining cars sold though 1972.

The most important model changes and improvements VW Porsche 914:

1969: Introduction of the VW-Porsche 914 at the IAA: four-cylinder boxer installed in the center, removable Targa roof. Presentation of Porsche 914/6: six-cylinder engine, five bolt wheels, 250 km/h speedometer, chrome-plated bumpers, 8000 rpm tachometer, electrical wiper/washer, three-speed wiper motor. Targa roll-bar covered in vinyl.

November, delivery of Porsche 914/6 begins.

1971: August, modifications to electronic fuel-injection system. Rear skirt shortened, with vertical air inlets. Interior modified: coat hook on right, additional center windshield air vent. Modified switch for concealed headlights and modified ignition lock. Distributor changes. Optional: 5.5 x 15 wheels (steel or alloy). 165 HR 15 tires. Option package M 471: Wider fenders, front and rear stabilizers, 7" wheels with 185/70 tires.

1972: August, Porsche 914/6 dropped.

Four-cylinder models: additional air vents on left and right of dashboard; door panels covered with basket-weave material. Passenger seat adjustable, switch for wipers and washer on steering wheel. Modified steering column. Engine modifications: (fine-tuning).

1973: August, introduction of Porsche 914/2.0: 1971 cm^3, 100 DIN hp @ 4900 rpm, fuel injection. Porsche 914/1.7 still offered. New engine mountings, different dry air filter. Improved engine compartment noise insulation. Insulation mat even in rear trunk. Suspension softer, shorter rear skirt.

All models: matte-black bumpers, black insignia. Interior: passenger footrest. Headliner design matches seats. Black handles and window cranks, new shift guide. 250 km/h speedometer.

Extra cost: comfort package (includes vinyl-covered roll bar, additional instruments in the center console, and velour carpeting among other things). Sports package: alloy wheels, front and rear stabilizers, halogen headlights, among other things.

1974: August, Porsche 914/1.8 replaces 1.7: bore 93 mm (previously: 90 mm), modified combustion chamber shape, redesigned intake and exhaust manifolds. 85 DIN hp @ 5000 rpm. Export models for North America: Bosch L-Jetronic fuel injection, Europe: dual carburetors.

All models: New road wheel design, modified interior. Standard automatic three-point belts.

US models: rubber buffers at the rear.

1975: August, safety bumper with integrated square driving lights. License plate lit from the side. US models: exhaust gas recirculation, California models come with catalytic converter.

Extra: plastic front spoiler

914/2.0 special GT edition: special colors: black/yellow and white/red.